The Spirit of Play

This book is dedicated to the memory of my parents, Marvin and Geneva, to my teacher Sogyal Rinpoche.

It is also dedicated to every person who is connecting with their spirit, the nature of their mind, or whatever you call your relationship to the underlying soul of all that is.

The Spirit of Play

Cooperative Games for all Ages, Sizes, and Abilities

Dale N. Le Fevre

Revised edition of "New Games for the Whole Family", originally published in 1988.
First published by Findhorn Press 2007.

ISBN: 978-1-84409-092-1

British Library Cataloguing-in-Publication Data.
A catalogue record for this book is available from the British Library.

Edited by Kate Keogan
Cover design by Brian Parkinson
Cover photo by John Birchard
Back cover photo by Sverre Koxvold
Drawing of the author, page 154, by Sanna Koski
Layout by Pam Bochel
Printed and bound in the USA

1 2 3 4 5 6 7 8 9 10 11 12 13 12 11 10 09 08 07

Published by
Findhorn Press
305A The Park,
Findhorn, Forres
Scotland IV36 3TE

Tel 01309 690582
Fax 01309 690036
email: info@findhornpress.com
www.findhornpress.com

Table of Contents

Last 19 Minutes

Traveling six days straight –
now down to those
last nineteen minutes
and wondering what
it's all about.
Am I crazy
or merely insane?
NOT insane!
so I must be
C R A Z Y.
Taxi Bus Boat
Taxi Train Boat
Train Train Train
Tram, not insane, man
not insane.

Dale

This poem was written on a journey from Jerusalem to Bochum, Germany, where I was presenting a workshop. I started with $30, a boat ticket, a Euro-rail Pass, and just enough money to make it.

I will ask you to do tremendously simple things.
    We've lost the art of dong simple things, everybody
wants something complicated. Some great target to reach,
some great goal.
    The biggest goal ever reached.
    It's hard sometimes, to do something simple like this.
You have to be children again.
You have to learn to walk again, because this does not lie
    on the ways of your education and your knowledge.
You have to be open to any crazy thing happening and not let
    the mind come in and say what are people going to think
    about what I'm up to now?
This is meaningless.
Let it be meaningless.
It's so simple.
Just drop the thoughts, so complex, so anxious and just be
    terribly simple . . .
And if you find it difficult to get started, then just stand
    there.
Breathe a little deeper than you normally do.
And when the movement starts to happen just become
tremendously
aware
of the movement, the
extreme edge of the movement,
as if you're standing on the front fender
of a train that's moving along the rails,
whhoosssh
and you haven't got time to watch
in advance, so fast
the view is always changing
and you are right there standing on the front of the train.

Michael Barnett

The teaching which is written on paper is not the true teaching.

Written teaching is kind of food for the brain. Of course it is necessary to take some food for your brain, but is more important to be yourself by practicing...

Shunryu Suzuki

A Personal Note From the Author

Quite often I'm asked how I got involved with playing and teaching cooperative New Games. The story is my own continuous miracle.

It starts in the Spring of 1974, when a psychic told me that by the end of the year I would be leaving my job and moving to the west coast of America. I had no reason to believe her, since I was very happy with my situation at the time. I lived beside a lake surrounded by beautiful countryside. My job as a Student Affairs administrator was well paid and fulfilling. I had a good rapport with the students and my supervisor had given me an extremely high evaluation. There appeared to be nothing that would cause my departure. In addition, I was becoming security conscious about holding on to my job since at that time work was getting difficult to find. I regarded the psychic's prophecy as a nice vision to hold (for years my secret desire had been to move to San Francisco), but not very likely to happen.

"How'd You Get Into These Games?" "By Getting Fired and Watching T.V."

However, in September, lightning struck. After getting off to a fine start, my supervisor started saying he wanted to fire me!

I was shocked. After a traumatic period lasting a few weeks, I decided to resign. Although I was shattered, I now began actively putting energy into the vision the psychic had given me: I wrote to about ten communes./ free schools in the western U.S. asking about living / job opportunities. Some replied though none inspired me, and I prepared unenthusiastically to choose one that might best suit me.

Then, one Sunday in late October, a ray of inspiration shone through my despair. Although critical of American commercial television generally, I was watching an excellent youth program called, appropriately enough, "Make A Wish." Indeed. During that day's show a five minute film clip called "New Games" answered my wish to find something that captured my imagination. What I saw were people of all ages playing together and having a ball. When it was over, I spoke aloud with wide-eyed enthusiasm, "That's what I want to do!"

Why Not?

The next day I phoned the T.V. network and they gave me the producer of the show, Peter Weinberg, in New York City. I asked him where the New Games people were located. He replied, "San Francisco." Perfect. Of all the places I could have gone, this was, as I mentioned, my first choice, though it had seemed unlikely I'd really be able to go there.

A short time later I sent a letter, resume, and picture to the New Games Foundation, a non-profit educational organization, asking them about work. Two months passed during which I heard nothing. For a time I forgot about it: then, just as I started to wonder if I should write again, a phone call came with the question, "Do you want to train with us?" "Sure!" A week and a long cross country drive later I arrived in San Francisco with only my backpack: my invitation was just for two weeks.

The first night I spent in California, I stayed with friends in Corona Del Mar, near Los Angeles. The next day, the first of February, a warm sun rose. We went to Laguna Beach, which featured tide pools with aquamarine sea anemones, bright purple sea urchins, and other beautiful sea critters. After having crossed a very cold continent in the heart of winter, all I could say was, "I'm not leavin'!" Somehow, I would find a way to stay in California, regardless of the length of my invitation.

"Open Your Golden Gate"

When I first arrived in San Francisco, I went straight to director Pat (now called "Rose") Farrington's home near the Haight-Ashbury district. I was "greeted" by two mangy, barking mongrel sheep dogs (ironically, the least intelligent one was named "Stewart," after Stewart Brand, the originator of New Games). Pat's children were there but they didn't pay much attention to me: it seems I wasn't the first visitor to turn up out of the blue. The flat was minimally furnished – what I would call a neo-hippie pad, which had just become my style. In any case, I was far too excited to get discouraged at this point.

Finally Pat arrived along with the Foundation staff, even though it was a Sunday. It was more like a family than a business. We went to the warehouse office where we, would you believe, played a bit! Whatever else might be said about those early days, we did play a lot whenever we needed a breather from work.

My vision of the New Games Foundation was very different from what I found. I had expected the well-organized ongoing concern that it later became. What I found was a loosey-goosey group with a lot of enthusiasm but little organization and even less money. In other words, no money. In fact, they were even borrowing funds to cover basics like rent and phone.

As the first week passed, I thought of how I could extend my stay. Just then, Pat told me that the only way to learn what New Games were all about was to organize a festival, and they just happened to have one planned for May. Nirvana! I tried not to show my excitement too much but readily agreed. The arrangement fulfilled both our needs – mine to do something I truly loved and hers to get a volunteer worker with a regular income. (At the time I was drawing unemployment benefits.) Thus began my new career as a New Games person.

Meet the "Creator"

Since then it has taken me to the brink of my most far-fetched fantasies. Along the way I've met some seemingly mythical people such as Stewart Brand, originator of New Games and editor of the Whole Earth Catalogue series and the *Whole Earth Review* (formerly *CoEvolution Quarterly*). I first got to really know Stewart after two years at the New Games Foundation when he called to ask if he could borrow our Earth Ball, a six-foot inflatable globe. He said he wanted to take it to Oregon for a "Poetic Hoo-Hah" featuring writer William Burroughs. When Stewart told me that the event organizer was Ken Kesey, author of *One Flew Over the Cuckoo's Nest* (whom I'd made a personal vow to meet one day) I replied, "Sure, you can have the ball. Can I come with it?"

Stewart agreed.

Later I learned that Ken was the fellow who had come up with the idea for the Earth Ball, which had since become a key symbol for New Games. He met us at the train station in a Pontiac convertible already holding six people, complete with a two-person video crew conducting a mobile interview while Ken drove. The fun had begun.

I've met many other mythical and magical people as well during my journeys presenting New Games. In my view, perhaps my most unlikely meeting was with Dr. Jonas E. Salk, discoverer of the polio vaccine, in Stockholm, Sweden, during the summer of 1982. Dr. Salk had been a legend to me ever since I was a child for, twenty-two years earlier, I had graduated from Jonas E. Salk Junior High in Rolling Meadows, Illinois! After I told Dr. Salk that I was traveling and teaching leadership of cooperative games, he commented to my friend, "We need more people doing things like that." This touched me deeply.

Next Stop

I have also traveled far and wide – so far I've presented New Games all over the U.S., in Canada, every major country in Western Europe, Greece, Poland, Israel, Egypt, South Africa, India, Japan, Australia and New Zealand. Sometimes my meals have been like this: a Danish pastry in Copenhagen for breakfast and Swedish meatballs in Stockholm for dinner. Although I'm not much of a sightseer, the most amazing things I've seen were the pyramids on the outskirts of Cairo *and* the Taj Mahal under a full moon in Agra, India – during the same week! This was never what a farm boy from Wisconsin thought he had in store for him.

I've been able to go to all of these places because people have recognized that games can be fun for everyone. That's my basic message, and most people are receptive to it. Once a person is involved in one of these games, their response is almost always positive. Cooperative games create a universal language with which people can relate to each other.

Players of all languages seem to enjoy New Games, even when the players don't speak each other's language.

People in various cultures I've been exposed to respond similarly to the games. While Scots, for example, were friendly and talkative, they found it difficult to touch each other. Nevertheless, after a half hour of games, this cultural taboo was much less in evidence. I had graded the games by the amount of touching involved so that the process of moving through cultural conditioning could be done in a series of steps, rather than all at once. In the Mediterranean countries and particularly in India, men hugged and women went arm-in-arm in public, but here there is a strong taboo against persons of the opposite sex touching openly. Again, this was largely dispelled after using the same "formula," at least when the games were played out of sight of the general public.

Israel presented a fantastic challenge: bringing Jews and Arabs together through play. It was only after I arrived that I realized that getting Jews to play with other Jews was an even bigger challenge. The difference in cultural backgrounds (they came from all over the globe) made the competitiveness between groups hard to overcome; on the other hand, the culture of the local Arabs is similar to that of Jews from Middle Eastern countries (Mizrahi Jews).

In practice, this meant everybody was talking at once, trying to be heard above the others. It made presenting games in my normal manner impossible – my game introductions were going almost unnoticed at the first games session I did at a Jerusalem community center. I realized that I was going to have to do something dramatic, and fast (!), to get the group's attention. Without time to think, I intuitively started flailing my arms and legs in the air and screeching like a maniacal monkey. It worked. ("Crazy" people are given attention all over the world since nobody knows quite what to expect.) As soon as I had everyone's attention, I started to introduce a game.

My main problem in Northern Ireland before the current peace was established was not getting Protestants and Catholics to play together but just keeping my composure while on the way to the play sessions. While driving through various towns, I saw squads of British troops suddenly appear with rifles in hand, apparently ready to fire at a moment's notice. Their steely glances pierced me. In this regard, my co-worker Eamon was no help, either. On our route he would casually point out all the gaping holes where buildings had been bombed. In some areas this was every third structure. I arrived at several sessions more in need of New Games than the participants.

Say What?!?!

Incidentally, I found that British English is almost 20 percent different from American English and that this definitely must be taken into account when communicating. I learned not to say, "Do you like my suspenders?" which is their word for garters! And I came to understand that when a gentleman asked me "Shall I knock you up in the morning?" he was not proposing to make me pregnant (I wondered just how he could do that!) but to come to call on me early the next day.

I have found that some real differences between people are closely related to their professions or roles in society. For instance, humanistic psychologists generally love body-contact games. (In fact, it's hard to stop them once they get going!) Business people are often the most enthusiastic players. Teachers usually do the things they tell their students not to do. Housewives are initially fairly reluctant to risk looking silly. People who are considered social outcasts, such as youth gang members and young prisoners, frequently come up with the most creative suggestions for changing games. But equally as often, groups surprise me with their response.

That makes it interesting for me – I must find and tickle a group's "funny bone," so to speak, or find a way of connecting with them. I have the belief that cooperative games will work with any group of people, and I'm always on the lookout for a group I know nothing about for a new challenge. This can mean going to a new country, such as I did in South Africa during apartheid and where I was invited to bring players of different races together; or new situations, such as playing with business people in normal business dress, as I did in Stockholm at a business conference. (I couldn't help but laugh when I saw them running crazily back and forth waving their arms in the air yelling "Wee-ooo, wee-ooo," pretending to be fire engines.)

I had one huge challenge when I was invited to a high school in Rochester, New York, to lead New Games with their teenage students in a gym class. After I was introduced, I asked the students to come down from the bleachers where they were seated to join me doing some of the games. Not one single kid moved. I knew I had to do something immediately or the event would be a fiasco. I leveled with them, saying, "Look, I came from a long way to be here; all I ask is that you try one game to see if you like it." With that, they came down and we ended up playing for the full time allowed. They had a ball! And so did I.

Germany was the first country where I tried to work using a language I did not know. I had one night to learn a little German and actually might have done better sticking to English. Due to my mispronunciation, "Make a circle" became "Make a crisis" (though perhaps this came closer to the truth of what really happened with my attempts to speak German). I found that mime, dramatic gestures, and translating the names of games gave participants a better sense of what was coming. There was some confusion, but presenting became a game in itself.

A big advantage for me has been that most Europeans understand a fair amount of English. It is a requirement in their schools because it is often used in business. In any case, those who understand can translate for those who don't.

How Playing Is for Me

My focus has gone from rediscovering playfulness to finding that the spirit of play is an invaluable part of my total spirit. It's a way to make contact with my true being. When playing New Games, I am totally present. I'm not thinking about whether my rent is due, or a relationship, or travel plans. I'm not aware of anything except what's happening in front of me at the moment. Being present is a major goal of meditation.

My life is becoming a game of spiritual discovery. The road is long, but the distance is short: I have only to look within. Pain paved the way for growth as much as joy. I've been learning how to work with energy and realize that there is no good or bad. There is just energy, and how I use it makes the difference in my life and determines how it comes back to me. The way I interpret it determines how it affects my life. For instance, getting fired from a job has first appeared like a catastrophe and left me distraught, but the times it has happened have led me to better situations that I liked more and served me better for fulfilling my potential. It is quite likely I would not have left my old jobs, though, if I hadn't received this push. As time goes on, I've come to judge less what happens, but rather to see where it leads. One door closing usually means another is opening. And the miracle of discovery continues!

There are at least two kinds of games. One would be called finite, the other infinite. A finite game is played for the purpose of winning, and an infinite game for the purpose of continuing the play.

The rules of a finite game may not change: the rules of an infinite game must change.

Finite players play within boundaries: infinite players play with boundaries.

The finite player aims to win eternal life: the infinite player aims for eternal birth.

James P. Carse

Introduction

"How often do NFL defensive linemen deliberately try to get the quarterback?"

"You always try to get a key player out of the game," said (Hanford) Dixon. "You want to do it legally," he added, "and we did it legally." (Referring to the known injury San Diego Charger quarterback Dan Founts suffered when hit on two successive plays by the Cleveland Browns.)

International Herald Tribune

Some people suppose that because competition and acquisition are used in the exploitation of others, enlightened people should follow the ideal of non-competition and non-acquisition. Many years ago, Anne Aitken and I taught in a private boarding school that was established on the principle of non-competition. It didn't work. The young people were not stretched; many became lazy; others found destructive, underground ways of competing.

Competition can be healthy. After all, conversation itself is a kind of competition, and at its best saves all beings. When the self is forgotten, the play becomes the thing, and everybody benefits. And as to acquisition, Gandhi, and the Buddha himself, had a few possessions. Competition sharpens our realization and certain possessions are adjuncts of life. At what point do they go wrong? ... Competition, acquisition, and possession go wrong when compassion is missing, when dana (charity) is disregarded.

Robert Aitken

The Spirit of Play is about just that. This book is designed to help you make play a part of your life. Games are not really necessary for this purpose. Spontaneous play is perhaps more fun than anything imaginable, but it doesn't always happen. Perhaps in your life, it rarely happens. Maybe it never happens. Since games have the magical quality of focusing people on playing, I am presenting this book as one way to help you get started. I want to emphasize that my goal is not merely to get you to play the games in this book, even though they are a good way to begin learning to be playful, but to assist you in finding playful ways to live, whatever situation you are faced with.

I have included advice, based on my experience, on how to present and use the games, but my first word of advice is: Don't believe everything you read. What worked for me may not work for you, and what I say won't work just might be the thing you needed to make it go. I think you will find my guidelines pretty sound in general, though.

A question that sometimes comes up is, "What is so different about these games?" Once you've played them, you'll have a good idea. To try to put it into words is nowhere near the same as the experience. However, having said that, this is discussed in the next part, *What's so Special About These Games?* Think of it as a road map – it's not the road itself, but it can help you to get where you are going.

Sometimes it's not the games so much as what you do with them. The difference is a matter of attitude, as conveyed through presentation, or of adapting to a particular group. Detailed guidelines are given on how to do this in the section called *How to Adapt Games.*

I've included games for a few players or for many, in three flexible levels of activity: quiet, moderate, and active (see *Contents*). Some name games are included so that players don't have to call "Hey, you!" all the time (naturally, in the *Name Games* section). Also, games for choosing teams are offered as a way of avoiding the unpleasant aspects of choosing sides in the section *Cooperative Games and Ideas for Making Teams and Choosing Partners*. Not one piece of equipment is required for any but the "newest" games in this book. For convenience, I've made lists of games to help teach various motor and perceptual skills (Developmental Skills), games to open and end play sessions, and a few Resources.

The spirit of play is always present. It is the child within us all.

We could never take anything up like ordinary children. We had to be perfect, to outdo all the other children in the neighborhood. So we had a coach for tennis, an instructor for riding and another for skating and another for swimming. Normally I would have enjoyed them all – but with father in the foreground urging us on there was no fun in any of it. Games of any kind became a duty and drudgery.

Buster Lloyd-Jones

The system starts here: I got 90 (at school) and my mother and father hug and kiss me, "Did so good, he got a 90! MMM, Kiss, Kiss." But that 90 don't mean anything unless you got a 20. And if I'm not a nut, and if 90 gets me loving and kissing, I hope you get a 20, man. I'm gonna hope you fail.

But later on I really jive myself and say, "May the best man win." May the best man your ass! I'm going to win out and get my kissing and hugging!

Yeah. The competitive system.

Lenny Bruce

To be playful is not to be trivial or frivolous, or to act as though nothing of consequence will happen. On the contrary, when we are playful with each other we relate as free persons, and the relationship is open to surprise; everything that happens is of consequence. It is, in fact, seriousness that closes itself to consequence, for seriousness is a dread of the unpredictable outcome of open possibility. To be serious is to press for a specified conclusion. To be playful is to allow for possibility whatever the cost to oneself.

James Carse

What's So Special About These Games?

First and foremost, these games are for everyone. That is, everyone who wants to join. I've played with a wide variety of people and have seen old folks and children hugging to become unfrozen from the "Wizard's" spell, families and singles getting all tangled up in a "Giant Knot," mentally and physically challenged people becoming "Fire Engines," police and prisoners protecting their mutual leader from the "Detective" – sometimes all these people were in the same game! It's hard for anyone to resist joining.

Some new games are ones you know but haven't played for years or that have been changed to make them new. Others are games you've never seen before, and still others are invented by you. Some games, like "Cat and Mice," are quite physical while others, like "Captain Video," are gentle and quiet. All are safe.

While a number of the games include competition, no one cares or remembers who wins or loses. There is no pressure or need to win; hence there is no anxiety about losing. People play a game *with* one another rather than *against* each other. Players are not eliminated: they simply change roles and keep playing. No special treatment is given when there is a winner: "You're the last one left? Great, you can start the next game."

Playing is just as exciting for someone who has played the games many times as it is for the first-time player. The games don't get boring because they are different each time you play them. I'm never sure what will happen! Some groups just take off in a unique direction with a game. Even though I've introduced some games more than a hundred times and think I know everything about them, players just being introduced to them can sometimes think of a wonderful variation that I've never tried or that has never even occurred to me.

By encouraging suggestions and responding positively to them, I invite everyone to use their imagination. Though rules are given to start a game, they are not chiseled in stone. Everybody's ideas count. Sometimes the ideas flop. So what? Who cares? At least we tried it. We can always go back to what we started with or try something else. Very often, though, we end up with a better game.

No Toys, Just Us!

Unlike many games or activities, all but three of the games in this book require no equipment. Gimmicky equipment is expensive and therefore not economically feasible for most people. There are other problems: stationary apparatus is generally accessible to small numbers, while equipment that can be moved always involves transport and scheduling, and all equipment requires maintenance and replacement.

The main ingredient in New Games is the player. People discover how much fun it can be simply to play games cooperatively with each other. A unique sense of community develops where people feel closely connected. They can let go of their normal roles in a supportive atmosphere that allows them to express themselves more freely.

Anyplace, Anybody

These games can be played almost anywhere. In reply to a question from Simon Vinkenoog, a Dutch author, asking whether I could do a few games in his cramped, crowded workroom at home, I blurted out confidently, "I can do them in a closet!" Although that may be a slight overstatement, there are games you *could* play in a closet.

An important aspect I stress is that each player develops a concern for the safety of fellow players so that everyone plays fully but no one is ever hurt or left out. This provides us with a model of cooperative behavior that is constantly reinforced during the games session. Since it doesn't matter who wins, and since by the very nature of these games, players are constantly changing roles or teams, there is little chance to develop animosity.

There are important psychological and sociological aspects to the playing experience. In games where there is no "loser," a person can develop self-esteem and a more positive self-image. There isn't the constant feedback of "You're not good enough." You *are* good enough. All you have to do is join the game.

It doesn't matter if you can't do the action, such as running; you simply do the best you can. No one is judging. Or you can always suggest a change, such as moving in s-l-o-w m-o-t-i-o-n. It doesn't destroy the game as long as the other players are included in making the decision. An alternative that is fun and a challenge can always be found. No one says, "You can't play. Go away!"

When playfully expressing oneself, one relaxes, often subconsciously, and tension dissolves. People who are normally shy, withdrawn or afraid of meeting new people regularly "forget" how they are supposed to be and play without inhibition.

Finally, basic exercises of any kind can be pretty boring boring boring, but when the exercise can be put in the form of a game, it can become an adventure. Since the elements of the games are highly adaptable, they can be changed to get the desired result. For instance, any motor or perceptual skill can be developed through the use of games. Many of these skills are already a part of most games, and it merely requires finding a game that has the desired movement, social skill, or discrimination. If one can't be found, you can invent a "new" game! (See the end of the book for listings of motor and perceptual skills involved in the games.)

Hints for Games Leaders

Games facilitation skills generally remain the same: concern for safety, playfulness, enthusiasm and a brief, clear description with a demon-stration are still keys to making a game work. However, a games leader outside her/his "territory" needs to be aware of local taboos, at least initially. Many of these, like not touching, generally melt away as the feeling of warmth increases between participants.

A facility in the art of mime, or at least dramatic gesturing, is of obvious value when presenting games to people whose first language is not the same as yours. Play leaders can also benefit from knowing a few key phrases in the players' language, e.g. "Make a circle," "Form a line," or "Get a partner," plus the name of the game translated.

So, how does it work for me? At first, it's generally the same. I walk into a room of nervous people who are very self-conscious about being there to "play." The thought crosses my mind, "How will I ever get these people to play?" Right. This is my ever-present challenge. The simple answer is to start by doing something I find fun that isn't too challenging or silly for the group. Or maybe I'll say something like, "I didn't know this was a funeral!" to help release the tension. Or maybe I'll throw a sponge Frisbee to an unsuspecting soul at point-blank range, thereby startling them (and, after they realize it's a sponge Frisbee and they didn't get hurt, causing them to laugh). Or I might put on a funny hat. Next, someone smiles, or if I'm lucky, laughs. The ice begins to melt and away we go.

Before beginning to introduce games, I always ask people to form a circle. This signals an informal ritual of beginning to the participants. Sometimes I ask people to close their eyes and remain quiet for a few moments to allow time to tune in to their own playful spirit, to each other, and to the place we are in.

Next, I'll present a game that isn't too physically or psychologically threatening like "Giant Knot," or, for kids, "Fruit Basket." If people appear stiff and tentative I stick to games that do not single out individuals because this embarrasses them too much. However, games that are *too* safe are boring – the risk-taking is also part of the appeal of a game.

As the group loosens up, each game becomes a little bit sillier than the last. Introduced at the right time, a very silly game is totally absorbing, even for a very serious group. It can cause a breakthrough

to truly open the assembly. For instance, people outside Germany told me that the Germans take everything seriously, but I was able to see their playful side, which is actually substantial. The goofy game of "Choo-Choo" – a "train" of people invites others to join them by making cheerleading chants, complete with jumping gestures, of the onlookers' names – was a very effective ice breaker at the German Sports Academy in Cologne. After that, they were ready for anything! Though the group was hesitant to speak initially, fearing they would make a grammatical mistake in front of me, they later began making jokes in English, which is difficult in to do in one's second language.

Share-a-Game

People often share new games with me. In fact, one-third of the games in New Games come from this source. For example, the game of "Quack!" comes from Englishman Jim McCritchie, whom I met in Geneva, Switzerland; the "Greeting Game" comes from Jeroen (pronounced Ye-ROON) of Eindhoven, Holland; "Cat and Mice" comes from a French boy I met at a workshop in Aseda, Sweden; and I learned A-Rum-Sum-Sum in Germany, only to find variations all over Scandinavia and the U.S.

Before You Start Playing

I have indicated a range of how many people can play each game, though usually the middle point is the best number of players. When you have more than fifty participants, or the maximum indicated, generally it is better to make two groups of the same game or two different games. The latter might involve an active and a quiet game, thus giving people a choice of what they can do. It becomes hard to have a sense of what's happening with too many people, and some games become boring or dangerous with too many participants. However, there are games that lend themselves to groups of more than fifty, and these are indicated as: 50+.

The rules of these games are provided as a starting point for playing. Use your own and your fellow players' ideas to introduce and play the games. If you want a challenge, your "game" for introducing each one becomes seeing if you can find a different way to do it every time.

• Ice Breakers – Games to Start

Energy

Knots / Giant Knot

A-Rum-Sum-Sum

Fruit Basket

Zoom

• Games for Closure

Lap Game

La Ba Doo

Car Wash

Dead Lions

Bear Hunt

"What I was going to say," said the Dodo in an offended tone, "was that the best thing to get us dry would be by a Caucus-race."

"What is a Caucus-Race?" said Alice; not that she much wanted to know, but the Dodo had paused as if it thought that somebody ought to speak, and no one else seemed inclined to say anything.

"Why," said the Dodo, "the best way to explain it is to do it." (And, as you might like to try it yourself some winter day, I will tell you how the Dodo managed it.)

First it marked out a race course, in a sort of circle ("The exact shape doesn't matter," it said), and then all the party were placed along the course, here and there. There was no "one, two, three, and away," but they began running when they liked, and left off when they liked, so it was not easy to know when the race was over. However, when they had been running half an hour or so, and were quite dry again, the Dodo suddenly called out "The race is over," and they all crowded round it, panting and asking "But who has won?"

This question the Dodo could not answer without a great deal of thought and it sat for a long time with one finger pressed upon its forehead (the position in which you usually see Shakespeare, in the pictures of him), while the rest waited in silence. At last the Dodo said, "Everybody has won, and all must have prizes."

Lewis Carroll

Omni: why is humor so important?

De Bono: Humor is by far the most significant phenomenon in the human brain because it demonstrates lateral thinking – the escape from the mundane perceptual path to another path. For example, an airline pilot goes for a medical checkup and learns he is in fact almost blind. Still, he wants to fly for another year to get his pension. When the doctor asks him how he's able to land the plane, the pilot explains that he uses the Jesus Christ method: "I point the nose down, and when the copilot screams 'Jesus Christ!' I level off."

Omni Magazine interview with Edward De Bono

Games / Gentle Games

Games for Your Bomb Shelter (Few Players)

At Kiryat Schmone, a border town with Lebanon in the Galilee area of Israel, my co-worker, Jan Spector, our organizer, Iris Mishaeli, and I were actually asked if we knew some games that could be played in bomb shelters, to help ease people's fears and help relieve the tension of waiting for the all-clear signal. A few months later on German television news, I happened to see a filmed news report of Kiryat Schmone under heavy Arab attack. The reality of our preparations struck home.

~ Energy (5 – 25 players) ~

Any time we play games, we need some energy, and this game will give us all we need to start. To begin with, we take each other's hands, forming a circle. The energy begins moving around the circle by means of a hand squeeze passing from person to person.

Pass it around one way, then the other. Then comes the first test – see if the group can manage to maintain two energy pulses going in opposite directions. That means one person will receive energy from both directions at once and will have to squeeze back with both hands to keep the two energy pulses going.

After managing this, propose a real test of energy – passing it with eyes closed! After about ten seconds, send two more energy pulses. If you're really devious, you may want to continue to add new energy pulses in less and less time – until you hear laughter (usually in a minute or less) – letting you know that there's enough energy to begin the next game.

~ ZOOM (5 – 25 players) ~

If you're sick of getting stuck in traffic jams, wishing you could just zoom past the motionless cars, here's a way you can – in your fantasies, at least.

After the group is in a fairly close circle, pass the word "zoom" around from person to person. It will likely go slow, so as it comes back to you again, you can liken the speed to first gear of a car. Ask the group to try again, a little faster, in second gear. Then third, and fourth. For sports car enthusiasts (and with a small number of players) you might even try fifth gear.

Finally, to make the "car" safe with all this speed generated, it must have brakes. To apply brakes, a player must stick his leg out and step down on an imaginary brake while uttering a braking sound (or screech) "E-e-e-ek!" (It's a good idea to have everyone practice this together – it can be embarrassing if a person is left to be the first one to make the sound all alone.)

After braking, the car not only stops but goes into reverse around the circle. It may be good to limit players to only one use of brakes so that all drivers get a chance to "Zoom" about. Otherwise, our car may get stuck on one stretch of road, and all the gear changes could wear out the transmission!

~ Zip, Zap, Pop! (5 - 15 players) ~

Snap, Crackle and Pop! were characters in an American advertisement for breakfast cereal. "Zip, Zap, Pop!" won't fill your stomach but will wake you up, since you have to be alert to play it.

We sit in a circle facing the middle. One person starts by placing one hand flat on top of her head with fingers extended towards the person next to her saying, "Zip." Whoever is sitting in the direction of where the starter's fingers are pointing goes next. It is recommended to go around the circle once doing this so everyone gets it by doing it.

Next, a person can either repeat the action of the starter by pointing in the same direction repeating the word "Zip," or he can reverse directions by placing his other hand flat under his chin pointing back in the direction he received the zip from while saying, "Zap." Practice this till the group gets the idea.

Like so many things these days, there is another possibility. The second person can also point at anyone in the circle and by saying "Pop," the person pointed at is next. From there on it's Zip, Zap, or Pop!

If anyone should (heaven forbid) make a mistake, for instance, zapping while making a hand motion for a zip, we do not eliminate him. We merely let him know he did it wrong with an "oo" or "ah" or whatever seems appropriate. Then the person who made the mistake starts the game up again.

Captain
Video

The game is most fun when you keep a regular tempo going, *at least* one direction a second. Of course, at the beginning it's good to go slow until everyone gets the idea of how the game is played. Later, just when everyone seems to have mastered this, suggest speeding up the tempo to twice as fast. While you may sometimes feel zapped, you will rarely be too pooped to pop.

~ Captain Video (3 – 20 players) ~

Since this game relies on a visual message, it probably ought to be called "Television." Bor-ing! *Captain Video* was the first television science fiction show that I saw about space adventure (way back before *Star Trek)* and the results of this game are pretty far out in space, so...the captain and his Space Rangers fly again!

In Captain Video, we pass a motion (sometimes with e-motion). The easiest way to do this is to arrange players in a circle and, after demonstrating the game, have them face away from the center. Have one person in the center play the Captain. The Captain starts by tapping a Space Ranger (second player) on the shoulder, which is the signal for the Ranger to turn around.

Captain Video then performs a simple movement, for instance, doing one deep knee bend while winking. The Space Ranger (I do like writing that) must pay close attention to detail because she must later duplicate this exact motion to the next Space Ranger. The Captain takes the first Space Ranger's place in the circle, but now faces in so she can watch the unusual changes her winking/knee bend goes through.

Each successive Space Ranger (there it is again!) repeats this process until it reaches the last Ranger. Then the last Ranger and Captain Video step into mid-circle facing away from each other and, at the count of three, do the motion at the same time, the Ranger doing what he thought he saw and the Captain doing what she originally did. The two are not usually recognizable as the same thing – in fact, they are usually ridiculously different. Have the two face each other and repeat, so they both can see the differences. Who knows? The sight might even make Darth Vader laugh.

~ Face Pass (2 – 25 players) ~

Are you tired of seeing the same old face staring back at you in the mirror? Here is a chance to change it! Arrange the players in a circle so that everyone can see each other. The presenter starts by making a strange or distorted face. When everyone has had a chance to see it, the presenter turns either to her left or right. The person on that side, after he gets over the shock, amazement or laughter, carefully copies the expression – much like a mirror – and then both face the center so all can see how successful his attempt is.

Finally, the second person changes his expression until he finds one he likes. He then repeats the process by passing his creation to the next person in the circle. Continue in the same manner in the same direction until everyone has had a turn. If you have a group of shy players, have a volunteer make a face and everyone can copy it. After seeing your distorted mirror image, you might not mind your old kisser.

Many Tired Players

~ Dead Lions (2 – 50 players) ~

It's been a rough day. Everybody's hyperactive, making you wish you could send them into hyperspace. You need a rest, fast! But you can't get away just now. You can either scream, or try playing "Dead Lions." Or do one, then the other.

In Dead Lions the idea is to play dead by remaining as motionless as possible. (Did I hear a sigh of relief?) Have all the players (or lions) except one – the "hunter" from the zoo – arrange themselves so that they are comfortable lying, sitting or whatever. Explain to them that they must play dead so that the hunter won't catch them. If they move and the hunter sees them, they are caught and must join the hunter and help him.

Breathing and blinking the eyes are allowed (thank goodness!) but not other movements. All eyes must be open and visible – and lions can't hide their faces in any way. You may want to allow lions to move their eyes so that they can see the fun, too. Also, if a lion can move and not be spotted, that's a challenge and a risk they can choose to take.

The hunters can do anything to get lions to move (within socially accepted means) except touch them or shout in their ears (no spitting, either!) You soon realize how hard it is to be silly when you try as a hunter and how easy it is when you are not trying as a lion. In any case, this game should provide a few minutes of relief to your poor addled brain. Maybe more, if everyone wants to play again.

～ A-Rum-Sum-Sum ～
(2 – 50 players)

To get most games started, it's necessary to explain some sort of rules. Not so with this one. All you need to do is say, "Watch me and join in when you've got it." This game can be done either sitting or standing.

First, there is a little ditty to sing. It helps to give the group the words, which go like this:

A-rum-sum-sum,
A-rum-sum-sum,
Goolie-goolie-goolie-goolie,
Rum-sum-sum. (repeat)

A-ra-men, a-ra-men,
Goolie-goolie-goolie-goolie,
Rum-sum-sum. (repeat)

Keep a steady beat. The melody doesn't matter too much – you can make one up. I'm assuming most of you are like me and can't read music very well, but I've included it anyway.

Now comes the hard part – the hand movements. As you proceed to sing out the tune of "A-rum-sum-sum," you slap your thighs with your hands for each syllable. For example, "A" (right hand slap on the right thigh) "rum" (left hand to left thigh) "sum" (right hand, right thigh) "sum" (left hand, left thigh). Repeat this. It's easier than it sounds. Next comes the "Goolie-goolie-goolie-goolie," while alternating hand slaps on your chest for each "goolie." Hang in there! We're over half way.

Follow this with "Rum-sum-sum back on the legs. Go through the same thing one more time. Then "A-ra-men, a-ra-men" (though young kids I played it with liked to change it to "top ramen" which they often

had for lunch) while deeply bowing with your arms extended for each A-ra-men, followed be another "Goolie-goolie-goolie-goolie, rum-sum-sum." Do this part, starting with "A-ra-men" over again to finish. Whew! That was much harder to explain than it is to do.

Now that you've read the explanation, you can see why it's easier to just do it and have everyone follow. As the group learns the chant, you can speed it up each time you do it until it looks like cheerleaders gone mad in triple time.

~ Ain't No Flies On Us ~
(5 – 50 players)

We're the good guys, right? We're so good, flies won't land on us. But you guys! Well, we don't know about that, and we'd like to tell you about it. We can do this by making two lines of equal numbers facing each other about 20 to 25 feet apart.

We, the good guys, start by taking a step toward your line and calmly, politely, and not very loudly reminding you of the "facts:"

There ain't no flies on us,
There ain't no flies on us,
There may be flies on you guys, but
There ain't no flies on us.

"You guys (which includes gals)" then take a step toward us and slightly less calmly and politely, and just a bit louder, return the same message.

We continue moving closer, step-by-step, exchanging this chant until we're a minimum of an arm's length apart, no longer calm or polite, loud and actively gesturing. After "you guys" have a last turn, we might finish by noting that, in fact, no one has flies on them. Then, suggesting that to show no hard feelings for these unwarranted accusations, we might give the person across from us a hug or at least a handshake. You'll feel much better for it – remember, it's only a game!

~ Ironing Board (10 – 50 players) ~

It's time for you and a friend to go out on the town, but wait! Your clothes have some wrinkles and neither of you has time to change. Not to worry, since by some miraculous coincidence you both happen to be wearing the very latest miracle fabric, which only needs smoothing out with the hands of your companion. So while you stand still, your friend slowly runs her hands over your clothes, stroking out all the wrinkles. There, all better!

Now it's your friend's turn. Not only will your clothes be smoother, but you'll also feel much closer to each other. If you have to warn the group about appropriate touching, they're probably not ready for this game.

~ Quack! (2 – 50 players) ~

Some days everything seems upside down. Everyone you meet looks and acts a little strange. "Quack!" leaves no doubt because it creates these conditions on purpose, but in a humorous way. In fact, it's one of the silliest games I know.

Everyone stands with his or her legs slightly apart. Then they let their bodies hang down from the waist so that they are doubled over with their hands holding on to their ankles or knees. While looking between their legs, the players proceed to walk backward. Every time two people touch, they get bum-to-bum, make eye contact through their legs and loudly and proudly proclaim "Quack!" to each other.

Then they move on to a similar encounter with someone else. This goes on for a few minutes until people regain their sanity (or lose their sense of balance) and stand upright again.

"Quack!" is a game I would hesitate to open a session with since it might prove too threatening to people who are not yet in a playful mood. Perhaps you can see why. Still, there are groups that are willing from the get go. In any case, once a group is ready, this game can really loosen everyone up. Be prepared for anything from the group after "Quack!"

Fitness is no fad. What was once a nation of farmers, then of workers, is now a nation of clerks. Clerks need exercise...

John Naisbitt

Sensible people get paid for playing – that is the art of life.

Alan Watts

Life must be lived as play, playing certain games, singing and dancing.

Plato

Can You Make a Living Teaching New Games?

I'm asked this question by well-meaning people at least once a week, often once a *day*, and *sometimes* once an hour. Not only do I *make* a living from New Games, it's a *way* of living. Although I find myself in a world that doesn't value playing just for fun, individual people sense something worthwhile in what I'm doing, and they respond by coming to play workshops, buying books, CD-ROMs, and DVDs, all which help support me. So the short answer is "Yes, I can."

However, if my work was only about games, I would have left if after the first few years. What I've found is that not only is the New Games concept an attitude in relation to play, it can also apply to work and life in general. This is not news to those who enjoy their work, but it appears to me that they are in the minority. From what most people tell me, I can only conclude they see their work choices as limited by set patterns they dare not depart from, much like a train on a track. They always have good reasons for maintaining the status quo: a family, job security or preserving a standard of living. I've had these excuses myself.

My question to these people is simple, "Are you happy in your work?" It's painful to hear them defend the lives they lead in terms of their responsibilities and fears. But I have to wonder how anyone can possibly give his best to another person or his work if he isn't taking care of himself and his dreams. There has to be a balance. Too often, reluctance to take a risk means becoming stagnant. I believe a little part of us dies then.

Changing my own attitudes about this wasn't easy. As I've already pointed out, I had to get fired to find New Games. In fact, I've been fired four times in all. Each time I already knew I didn't want to stay with the job, but I hung on for one reason or another. A rule of thumb I stuck to was finding something I liked better. These days I listen to my inner voice more and try to move to projects I want to do before I'm pushed.

I see my work now as an almost unlimited possibility for living out my most outrageous fantasies. My options are like those of a ship in space – I can go in any direction I choose! There are, however, only a few directions that lead me where I want to end up. What I am suggesting in part is being flexible to ever-changing circumstances, an openness to new ideas, and a willingness to take risks trying out these ideas. By attempting projects I've never tried before professionally – like writing this book; or co-producing my first video, CD-ROM, and DVD; arranging trips to far away places around the globe – my life is my personal example that little is impossible.

A Little Reality

This does *not* mean that every fanciful thought I have immediately becomes a reality. In my experience, hard work is needed to give physical expression to my dreams. To illustrate this point, I'd like to describe how the European edition of the original version of this book was created. Writing does not come easily to me. In fact, let it be said that starting from my birth on the farm, it was never expected that I would be writing books. Even when I went to college, the longest thing I had written was a 24-page term paper. Double-spaced. Envisaging what I wanted to do wasn't difficult, but it was seven years before I finally got my ideas into print.

When I eventually began writing I wrote intensively for several weeks, then took my efforts to Anne, my first editor. In essence, she said it stunk. I had tried to write about everything I thought I knew about, including some things I actually didn't know much about. Although she was right, my pride was wounded and I gave up writing. It was six months later before I had recovered sufficiently. And when Per, who eventually helped me produce the first edition in English, subsequently asked me, "Why don't *you* write a New Games book?" I was able to say, "Yeah, why not?

The conditions I set for myself were that I had to have enough time and money plus an island retreat where I could do my writing. The latter was more a romantic idea than a requirement. Six months later I had all three on the island of Crete, Greece. It was idyllic – I had a place a mile and a half from the nearest town, Sitia, and it was 100 yards from the sea. After a week of eating Greek salads, drinking the local firewater called *raki*, and generally partying, I realized I had no more excuses. That scared me. What if I couldn't write well, like before? Finally, I thought, what the heck, I don't want to look back someday and say "I *could* have done it if I wanted." I wanted. So I gave it a try. The worst that could happen was that I'd find out I wasn't a writer, and that wasn't news to me, anyway. Well, OK, I'm not a natural writer, but that's what editors are for.

I started writing longhand, and after a week, I realized I didn't know how I was doing. It was then I discovered that Ray, a community member, was a writer and offered to help edit what I had written. I wrote and we edited until I had a first draft. I found a student who was visiting the island and paid her to type a draft, single-spaced (to keep the mailing cost low) to mail to my German publisher. Much to my surprise and delight, my publisher said that they were interested in publishing the book! As it turned out, I added other parts and had other editors in other parts of the world – I was on the move quite a lot at that time.

A year later, after many revisions, the manuscript was ready. However, despite my best efforts I could not find a publisher for the English version. From somewhere deep inside me I got the feeling that I should take the money that was supposed to get me through the winter and use it to publish the book myself. I decided to meditate and ask whether it was right to go ahead and publish the book myself. I got a strong, emphatic answer: "Yes!" Logically, this didn't make any sense whatsoever. Finding work, and thus income, is normally very hard for a New Games workshop leader in the winter months. I didn't even have a book distributor. But if I didn't find one I wouldn't be out in the cold; if the book flopped I could stack the unsold cartons of books in the shape of a room and live in it. (I'm only kidding. I think.)

Finally, three months after the book was printed, Element Books in Britain ordered 500 copies. A few months' later distributors in New Zealand and Australia did the same. It was not yet a big success, but at least it wasn't a failure.

The whole story was about to reveal itself. I still wanted to publish in my home country, the USA. After 20 rejections (some came with really nice letters about how the person truly liked the book, but it "didn't fit" in their list), I had tried, at last, to go to the company that had done the original "New Games Book" in the USA, thinking that since they had done one before, they would at least listen to the idea. At the Frankfurt Book Fair mentioned earlier, one of their representatives uttered the familiar refrain that it didn't fit their list, which was weird because they had published the original "New Games Book" and "More New Games," but finally I connected with someone who was positive and seemed to be working to get it done. In the end, after a year of trying, he said the company had been bought by a British publisher and that they were now only interested in best sellers. Which mine was not. But, he said he knew a fellow at another publisher, Putnam's, and that if I wanted, he would send the book over to him.

When I called the guy, Gene, I was all set to bombard him with all the reasons for him to take the book. After all, with 20 rejections, I was thinking I had to rev up my sales pitch. Much to my surprise, his first words were, "What a great book!" The book had sold itself. Finally I had my American publisher. Eventually, there were not only versions in the USA, but also in Germany, Sweden, Denmark, and France.

When I began, though, I didn't know for certain that I could sell more than a hundred copies. There were never any guarantees along the way. All I had was a trust from my inner knowing that it was the right thing to do. Even if it hadn't done well, I had fun watching it grow and take shape as a book. I felt like it was my first "child."

Me Now

In essence, I live my life as a New Game, a theme I explore in more depth in a chapter of this book called *Life Is a New Game.* This is what I've realized as I've explored different directions that I could take with the games, both geographically and professionally, and also personally and spiritually. When I am truly in touch with myself, everything seems to work out – even things that appear awful at the time.

What I have to remember, no matter what happens, is to keep telling myself "This story has a happy ending." My job is to find it.

I've found out why people laugh. They laugh because it hurts... because it's the only thing that'll make it stop hurting.

Robert Heinlein

Moderately Active Games

Games for Your Living Room (Few Players)

~ Car-Car (2 – 50 players) ~

To continue the theme of cars we started in "Zoom," here's a more active game where players actually can do some driving, even those who don't hold a license.

"Car-Car" starts by having people find a partner of about the same height, one in front of the other, facing in the same direction. The front player is the car. He places his bent arms about waist high in front of himself with palms out and open to act as bumpers, which he may need, since his eyes will be closed. The driver will guide her car by the steering wheel (shoulders) nimbly through traffic with no collisions (we hope). After all, insurance rates are high enough, and if you have an accident, they skyrocket!

After drivers take their cars for a little spin, have everyone freeze and reverse roles with their partner. If you don't have an even number of players, one person can be linked behind the driver as a passenger or back seat driver. Or you can ask them to invent a vehicle for three people. Sometimes two vehicles can come together to form trucks. What else can be made?

Yes, children will often try to run in to each other. You can always have a person or two assigned to be traffic cops who can stop them and give them a ticket, or have the offending vehicle go to the repair shop. Either way, it slows them down, and it's much more fun to stay a part of this game.

~ Car Wash (5 – 25 players) ~

(Suggestion: for more than 25 players, make another car wash or it will take too long to get to each player.)

Naturally, since we've been "Zoom"-ing our cars around in "Car-Car," they have gotten a little dirty. What they need is, of course (!), a "Car Wash." Have players make two equal lines facing each other, about one arm's length across. Then, assuming you're on a safe, dry surface, everyone kneels, though you can do it standing. One person, presumably you if you're introducing the game, goes to one end of the lines and announces what kind of car she is, "I'm a dirty old VW camper van," for instance. Then she proceeds down between the two lines on her hands and knees (or a bit bent over, if standing up), imitating the car she's chosen.

What kind of car you are and the condition it's in will determine the amount of cleaning done. The above camper van would receive a thorough scrubbing while a "new" Bentley would be treated most gently.

Meanwhile, the players in the lines do all the things a real car wash would do (but with fingers and hands, not sprayers and brushes), such as spraying soap and water, scrubbing dirt away, wiping the water off, and blow drying to finish the car. At the end we have a clean, well-scrubbed car. Remind washers to adapt to the different makes of cars and not get too vigorous or they'll scratch the paint and the owner will demand a refund!

The concept of this game was a little difficult to convey in Israel, where there were (at that time) no car washes! So we invented the first car massage machine.

~ Pyramids (6 - 21 players) ~

Windmills are a common sight on the horizon in Denmark and in some parts of California. New we can add pyramids as well, no matter where we live. One way to do this with no expense and with the fastest possible construction time is by using people. Forget automation and plastics. This game is labor intensive. You will need enough people so that you can form rows with a least one more person in each row than the row before, for example, 1, 2, 3, 4, and 5. The rows of people stand behind each other. The bottom row is the largest and heaviest while the top row is comprised of one light person. Have a row of "heavies" lie down on their stomach, side by side, close together, heads in the same direction. Each succeeding row lies on top of the last until one person lies on top of all. From experience, I've found that twenty-one is about the maximum number that can be in one pyramid without squashing the foundations. Also watch out for the person who sneezes!

~ The Greeting Game ~
(4 – 30 players)

"Hello, how do you do? Good to meet you" is a familiar greeting when we meet new people. It's a pretty mindless, if accepted, ritual. Here's a chance to change all that. In the "Greeting Game" we do what's unfamiliar. No words need be said. We start on our hands and knees. As we meet someone, we can greet him or her in whatever way we feel at that moment.

It's best not to think about it. Just do it. It could be a purr accompanied with a feline rub, a computer tunneling under a bridge, a gymnastic team from Ringling Brothers Barnum and Bailey Circus, or it could be as simple as a silent nod on a cold dark night. Whatever happens, happens (within legal and moral bounds!)

A group definitely needs to be loose for this game or it'll scare them away. If they're ready for it though, the "Greeting Game" can help bring a group to a highly playful level. Who could be reserved after greetings like this?

Games for Your Front Yard
(Many Players)

~ Little Ernie (3 – 50 players) ~

This is a story about Little Ernie and his baby brother, big sister, mother, father, grandmother, grandfather, dog (Bonzo), cat (Preston), and anybody else you want to throw in. (That is, if you have enough players to assume all the roles.)

However many roles you choose, divide the group into lines with that number of people in each line. For instance, if you have five people in the family, make lines with five people – er, family members – in them. Assign roles according to a person's place in line – that is, the first person in each line is Little Ernie, the second is baby sister (or who/whatever you choose to be second), and so on. Generally the lines are parallel with space enough for two to pass between them.

The story of Little Ernie doesn't exist yet, which is why you need a storyteller who can make up a story. Each time the storyteller mentions a player's role, that person must run around his or her entire line. If the "whole family" is mentioned in any way, they must all run around themselves. While running, players are encouraged to act out the story.

The tale is usually short – only a few minutes long – but what an action-packed thriller it turns out to be!

Little Ernie

~ Detective (10 – 50 players) ~

There's a gang on the loose in your neighborhood! Don't worry, though – they're easy to locate since they form a circle and, if their leader can be found, the gang can be stopped. We have sent a detective or two in the middle of the action to conduct the search. He closes his eyes while the gang leader is silently chosen from the circle.

The gang boss starts by making a motion – something everyone can do. Gang members try to hide their boss by copying every motion he makes. The detective(s) open their eyes and try to find the leader to put a stop to the gang's activities. The gang leader is encouraged to change the motion often, about once every 10 seconds, to give the detectives a chance. To add to the suspense, you can give the detectives three chances to find the leader. Once the leader is discovered (or if our Sherlock Holmes is out of luck), he is offered the detective's job. Such is the way of modern justice.

~ Bear Hunt (5 – 50+ players) ~

Bird watching has its exciting moments, no doubt, but let's face it, there can't be much of an adrenaline rush to it. Therefore, for the strong of heart I'd like to suggest a bear hunt. We don't hurt any bears; we just look for one to watch.

First, after seating our hunting party in a circle, we need to "march out into the woods." We can simulate this marching by alternating hand slaps to our thighs, left, right, left, right. Then, the expedition leader can call out a song that the hunting party then repeats, line for line:

> *Goin' on a bear hunt,*
> *Gonna find a big one,*
> *Gotta keep movin',*
> *It'll be fun!*

On the way through the woods, we encounter some situations: a bridge, tall grass, a mountain, and a swamp. With each new situation comes a new verse, as the tempo picks up:

> *There's a (1, a bridge; 2, tall grass; 3, mountain;*
> * 4, a swamp) up ahead,*
> *Can't go under it,*
> *Can't go around it,*
> *Gotta go (1, 3, over; 2, 4, through) it.*

After each situation is described in verse, it is acted out in mime. The "bridge" is crossed by making hand or foot slaps to the floor; grasping high in the air with the arms crosses the "mountain"; "tall grass" is swept aside by sweeping arm movements in front; and the "swamp" is gone through with the arms representing the legs squishing through the muck.

Finally, we see a cave! Slowing our "march" down, we start our final verse:

> There's a cave up ahead.
> It's all dark inside.
> Here's something furry…
> And BIG!
> With SHARP POINTED TEETH!!!
> OH! IT'S A BEAR!!!

Again we mime each line. For the first line, we slow the tempo, as if we are approaching a cave carefully. For the second, we reach out with our arms blindly searching. For the third, we find a patch of fur, which in the fourth line we discover is part of something large, as wide as our arms can stretch. Next we find some teeth with the tip of our index finger.

Upon discovering it's a bear, we rush away using triple-time march hand slaps, meeting with the situations we encountered coming in, but in reverse order: swamp, mountain, tall grass, and the bridge. Finally we march swiftly and safely home. Maybe next time we might consider bird watching, after all.

~ Blind Run (5 – 25 players) ~

Life has so much excitement and fear, and so many mysteries and obstacles, that it seems we're running blind at times. In "Blind Run," you literally experience this. The thrill and anxiety are not overwhelming, though. The unknown is fun and the barriers gentle.

Players form two lines facing each other, about six feet apart. They have their hands in front of them to straighten the course in case our blind runner goes astray on the path of life. At one end of the lines are at least two people who are prepared to bring a blind run to a gentle end by patting the runner on the shoulders and hips with their hands. These two *must* pay attention to the runner.

At the other end of the line is the runner, who naturally *enjoys* the thought of sprinting full speed with her eyes closed (until she tries, that is). Most likely everyone will want a chance to know the unknown this way, maybe even more than once, spinning around down the course or even running it backward!

The Enter-Scandinavia-and-Give-a-Workshop Game

For you see, so many out-of-the-way things had happened lately, that Alice had begun to think that very few things indeed were really impossible.

Lewis Carroll

My first trip to Scandinavia in 1980 was like playing a continental-sized board game. As the date approached to leave Amsterdam, Janet Spector (who was my working partner traveling with me at the time, as well as my significant other) and I discovered our first "turn" landed us on the "bad-steering-on-your-newly-purchased-VW-van" square. Every time we hit a bump in the road, the van, whose name was Arthur van Green, reflecting his Dutch origin and color, would wobble. This meant we had to draw a "repair" card with mechanic Anthony, the friend who sold Arthur to us. Anthony was a good mechanic but a little slow in carrying out his work. Meanwhile, time was running short.

Finally, everything was fixed so that we could go on to our next move. After traveling through Holland and (then West) Germany, we came to our first "ferry crossing" square on our way to Denmark. Next we landed on a square called "Customs" in Rodby.

Our main concern about Customs up until this point was how to smuggle seven bottles of alcohol we planned to give away as gifts. As we pulled Arthur up to the Customs checkpoint, the customs agent, who came out of his office to check us, was shaking his head as if to say, "No." This boded ill fortune. He started to check Arthur over thoroughly, finally insisting that one tire didn't have enough tread on it.

Move Back One Space

We reluctantly started to change the tire when the agent really began freaking out: it looked like we had just drawn a "return-to-West-

Germany" card. Unbeknownst to Jan and me, whoever had owned the van before Anthony had taped over some rust spots on the panels nearest the ground and painted over them. Our trusty agent discovered this and began to tear away the tape, proclaiming loudly, "Your van is finished, kaput! Return to Germany!" We were stunned. We had absolutely no expectation that this would happen, and we had to give a workshop in Stockholm in two days. We felt pretty bad.

At this point, we drew the "agent-is-human" card. No, he did not let us go into Denmark. However, Jan had lost a contact lens, and I told the agent we needed to look for it before we left. He said, "Oh, I'll help you look." Immediately he found it, while we had been unable to. So even though he was kicking us out of Denmark, we were able to experience his human side.

So, moving one square back, we returned to "ferry crossing" and went back one more square to West Germany. While on the ferry, we needed to complete our "repair " card, which was to finish changing the tread-worn tire. As I started to jack up our van, I heard this sickening crunch. While Arthur's frame was good, the places holding the jack were rusted to the point of uselessness. Nothing seemed to be going right. In the end we were able to use a hoist at a gas station, which was in fact much easier anyway.

Detour

The next move of our game was to find an alternative path to Sweden, since Denmark was clearly out. Looking at the map, I saw there was a direct ferry from Travemunde, West Germany, to Sweden. However, after checking the prices, which were exorbitant, I took another long look at the map and discovered a place called Sassnitz. This looked much closer to Sweden, and we figured it would be much cheaper. So we proceeded in the direction of Sassnitz without checking the map very carefully.

Shortly after leaving Travemunde, we came to a West German border guard. This struck us as peculiar, but we rationalized it by thinking it must be because Travemunde was a port town. It was not until we left the guard station and saw the barbed wire fences and soldiers with machine guns that it occurred to us that we were entering *East* Germany, which was where Sassnitz was. Once again, it was time to land on the square called "Customs."

Welcome, Comrades!

The first things the border guard asked for were our passports and car papers. After a frantic search, we discovered these were missing. We apparently had forgotten them at the West German guard post. Oops! This was *not* the best way to make our first entrance into an Eastern Bloc country. Though these countries are friendly now, at the time there was a bitter feeling between the governments of the East and West, reflected harshly in how officials treated outsiders. And these guys were quite armed. I had sudden flashes of spending the rest of my life in jail, with no one in the West knowing what had happened. It did not seem unrealistic at the time. Fortunately, at this time we once again drew the "agent-is-human" card and were allowed another draw for the "return-to-West-Germany" card. We drove back, picked up our papers, and got a transit visa to Sassnitz.

The novelty of the East German path to Sweden started with *three* searches of our van and paying a fee to enter. The road was winding and not lit, with few road signs to guide us, and about every 50 kilometers there was a checkpoint. None of this occurred in other countries. "Lead foot" Jan like to speed and totally missed a 90 degree turn that wasn't marked or lit, nearly causing us to crash. We also were nervous wondering if we would be arrested when we pulled the van over in a deserted spot to have a sleep for the night. We were sure that wasn't officially allowed. However, we had drawn a "good luck" card, and survived intact and free.

Goodbye, Comrades...?

For the last time, we thought we were moving onto a "ferry crossing" square, but this one had an East German twist. It actually read, "Lose ten turns, wait three hours." Although we arrived fifteen minutes before a ferry was to depart, which normally would have been plenty of time, when we asked the border guard, "Can we get on that ship?" he just looked at us and slowly shook his head as if to say, "No way." We didn't understand this and thought perhaps there wasn't really a boat leaving at that time. But there was. No explanations. The guard only said you had to arrive an hour and a half before the next boat.

So there we were, stuck in beautiful downtown Sassnitz, which wasn't so bad, really. Well, let's put it this way, it had an ice cream shop, which made Sassnitz a garden spot in any country, as far as I was concerned. It also gave us the opportunity to see briefly how East Germans lived, which was quite interesting since we had not encountered this or any Eastern bloc country before. You could say we drew a "cultural-enrichment" card.

It was our turn to move again, and we found out exactly why we were not allowed on the last ship and why we had been told to arrive early. Once again, we found ourselves on the "Customs" square. Arthur was put through three more security checks, and these were very thorough. They checked our gas tank by putting a wire down it, and our New Games brochures were closely scrutinized with many questions being asked. Since old Arthur was stuffed with bags and boxes of our things, this process took a long time. They didn't seem to mind the taped panels, though.

If You're Blond, This Must Be Sweden!

Finally, we got to the "ferry crossing" square. During the voyage, Jan and I glued the tape over Arthur's rusty lower panels. Earlier, when we had tried to enter Denmark and had told the border guard we were on our way to Sweden, he had replied, "Oh, they won't let you into Sweden, either." So we were nervous that we would once again be pushed back onto the "ferry crossing" square.

As we drove Arthur to the "Customs" square in Trelleborg, Sweden, we received a positive shock. This time we were greeting by beautiful blond ladies with smiles on their faces. Nobody asked a single question about our van. They couldn't have cared less. The lady agent who checked our van merely made a superficial perusal, all the while chatting merrily with us about the United States and San Francisco. She didn't even notice any of our six extra bottles of liquor. So, into Sweden we go! But wait. The game is not quite finished.

The "Lose Instructions" Card

After driving for a while, deliriously happy to have finally made it into Sweden, we decided to call the youth hostel where our host had made a reservation to tell them we wouldn't be able to make it that night. We discovered we had just drawn a new card in the game called "Lose Instructions."

After we had made a call from Travemunde the day before, we had left the sheet of paper with the name and phone number of the youth hostel and the name of the contact person for our games session. Suddenly, we didn't know anything! At this point, I became very depressed. Or, more accurately, pissed off.

Rather than keep playing the game and look for a solution, I chose to get upset and blame Jan for leaving the information sheet behind.

Fortunately, Jan kept playing – she drew a "Take-a-Chance" card, deciding the only thing we could do is call all the youth hostels in Stockholm to see if they had a reservation for us. Then we could only hope that our contact person would call the youth hostel to figure out what happened to us.

Remember, This Story Has a Happy Ending

Jan called all of the numbers she had been given by the operator, and none of them had a reservation for us. There was one place that did not answer. Not knowing what to do, we drove on, holding on to the thought "This story has a happy ending." It was all we had left. At four in the morning we finally had to stop to sleep.

We had planned to get up at six, but we slept right through the alarm until seven, when luckily we woke up. Back on the road we stopped again to call as we entered the outskirts of Stockholm. Once again we asked the phone operator for all the numbers of youth hostels to see if perhaps we had missed one. The very one that we couldn't get through to the night before had a different number from what Jan had written. This time when we tried it, we found – at last! – it was the right place.

The people at the hostel were incredibly friendly. They gave Jan a long detailed description of how to get to the "youth-hostel" square, laboriously spelling out the strange sounding (for us) names of the streets that all seemed about eighteen letters long. When we got there, they even let us take showers, though we hadn't spent the night. We were informed that Sten, our contact, *had* called the night before and even that morning. However, since the hostel staff didn't know who we were, and not having heard from us, they could give him no message.

We made a call to the host of our whole Swedish tour, Nic Nilsson, hoping to connect with Sten that way. Nic was out, so we left a message, "Jan and Dale called." It began to look like the end of the line. Our session was to begin at nine thirty and it was already eight thirty. Close, as they say, only counts in the game of horseshoes. Our only remaining hope was that Sten would make one last try to reach us.

So, having done all we could, we went downstairs to have breakfast. If the game was over, at least we'd finish on a full stomach. Up until this point, Jan had been the one who had been saying, "Oh, I have a strong feeling everything's going to be all right. We don't need to worry." I was the one freaking out. At this point, we reversed roles: Jan began losing hope while I miraculously relaxed and said, "Hey, it's going to be alright. You *said* it's going to be all right, and it will be." This calmed Jan.

Meanwhile, we tried Nic's office again. We were informed that while Nic wasn't there, and Sten hadn't called either, someone named Jan Daly had called about New Games. Figuring that here was someone who was interested in our workshop and maybe had a clue where it was supposed to be held, I called the number. At that same time the phone across from me at the registration desk of the hostel began to ring. When the man on duty answered, I discovered I was speaking to him. "Jan Daly" calling *about* New Games was in reality Jan and Dale *from* New Games: We had answered our own message! This provided a moment of lightness and laughter that had been sadly lacking in this "game," even if it brought us no closer to our workshop.

Better Late...

We were just finishing breakfast when the man at the desk rushed downstairs to tell us there was a phone call. I flew up and found, with great relief, it was Sten. As we had hoped, he made that one last try before calling the whole thing off. The time was nine fifteen. Looking back, this became one of many close calls and last minute connections I've had in my life.

Sten picked us up and we gave one of our best workshops, perhaps because we were overjoyed from completing our "Enter-Scandinavia-and-Give-a-Workshop" game successfully. Or maybe it went well because of the fact that we were outside. It was a sunny May day, and anything done in Sweden under these conditions has a hard time failing. We didn't care why. This game, at least, was over. And, once again, it proved that every happy ending does have a story.

Everything is funny as long as it is happening to somebody else.

Will Rogers

Active Games

Games for Your Rumpus Room (Few Players)

~ Three's a Crowd ~
(6 – 30 players)

There's an old saying that goes, "Two's company, three's a crowd." This is certainly true in the game of "Three's a Crowd." First, form a circle of pairs, one person behind another, facing the center. Then choose an "It" and a "Runner." This is a tag game. No one can stay with more than one other player (that is, a threesome) for longer than a few seconds at a time. The Runner, chased by the It, can join any twosome by standing in front of the pair, but the player farthest from the new arrival, who is in back in this newly created threesome, must suddenly "remember" an important matter elsewhere and dash off.

The new Runner is now pursued by the player who is It. When the new Runner is tired or just wants to change, he can stop in front of another pair, thereby making the person in back the third, or the One Too Many, and, therefore the new Runner. If at any point the It catches the Runner, the roles are reversed. The new It must count to three to give the new Runner a fair chance to escape. Allow players to go on the outside of the circle only, at least initially.

You can add to the excitement by making the rule that when anyone yells "switch," the pursuer (It) and the pursued (Runner) change roles. This keeps anyone from being stuck as the It for too long. Or you can also allow the It to join a twosome, passing on her role of It to the third person in back.

Whatever you do, "Three's a Crowd" is a game that can go on for a long time with many short-term meetings of twosomes. After all, getting to know many people a little bit is better than not getting to know anyone at all. Don't you think?

~ Fruit Basket (7 – 50 players) ~

Although this game isn't strictly for fruitarians, we have only our fruit basket with us for going to market. (As I've traveled in many lands, this game helped me learn the names of at least this one food category.) Every player except one sits on a chair (or something, like a pillow, jacket, carpet square, to designate their place), and the chairs / markers are in a circle. The person who is going "shopping" stands in the middle. We ask around the circle and everyone, shopper included, declares what kind of fruit they like the most. It's okay to have more than one of a certain kind of fruit (e.g., 2, 3, 4 or more apples).

The shopper starts his shopping by calling out the names of some of the fruits that were chosen, like apple, pear, and grapefruit. There are no limits to how many names he can call. When he says "switch" at the end of his list, all the people who have picked the fruit called out must leave their places and go to some other place made free by someone else who had to move. The shopper, weary from the day's shopping, seeks a seat on which to rest, too.

One person will not find a place to sit, as you may have gathered, since we have one less place to sit than the people playing. She becomes the new shopper and calls out fruits. After a few rounds, the Shopper can call "Fruit Basket," and everyone must change place (no fair coming back to your own place or even going to the seat beside you – too easy, fruitcake!). With this addition, the game looks something like a performance by Mexican jumping beans.

This game had such a profound effect on one lady in Chamarande, France, that she became know by her game name, passion fruit. I can't personally say whether she deserved the nickname.

Fruit
Basket

~ La Ba Doo (5 - 50+ players) ~

You can't dance? No matter – this is a crazy dance where no one will ever notice. We start by making a circle with our arms on our neighbors' shoulders. Now try sidestepping to the right on the beat, left foot following the right after half a beat. Finally, add the melody, which is the same as "Mary Had a Little Lamb," keeping time with your steps.

A stamp of the left foot should accompany the "Hey!" then we reverse direction repeating the song. After finishing this, whoever's introducing the game can ask the group, "Have you ever done the La Ba Doo dance?" They should answer, "Yes!" If their answer isn't very enthusiastic, ask again. Next the presenter continues by asking, "Have you ever done the La Ba Doo dance with hands on your neighbors' shoulders?" "No," should be the reply, since they haven't done it yet. "Let's try it," says the presenter, putting each of her hands on the shoulders of the two people beside her.

This pattern can be repeated with a number of possibilities such as hand on head, finger on ear, finger on (not in!) nose, hand on stomach, hand on knee, and, for the truly daring (not to mention flexible), hand on ankles, to name a few. You can repeat this dance at least five times with the above variations before people have had enough. The really fun part is making a ritual of asking the dancers after each dance if they have done each of the previous variations before asking about the new one, like so: "Have you done the La Ba Doo dance?" "Yes!" "Have you done the La Ba Doo dance with hands on shoulders?" "Yes!" "Have you done the La Ba Doo dance with hands on head?" "Yes!" "Have you done the La Ba Doo dance with finger on ear?" "No!" "Well, let's give it a try!"

As you can gather, very little dancing skill is required, merely the desire to have a good time together.

~ Fire and Trust Leap ~
(7 – 25 players)

We hear fire engines 50 floors below us in our high rise building and we wonder where the fire is. So we go to the window and IT'S IN OUR BUILDING! Quick, grab the kids, walk to the door and open it, walk down the hall for the stairs, go down the stairs, (remembering not to panic or run into other people), go over to a window and open it, get on the window sill and leap into a safety net.

Actually, we're miming all these motions, which is an elaborate way to lead into the next game of "Fire" and "Trust Leap." Arrange players in two lines facing each other an arm's length apart. Have the people in each line stand shoulder to shoulder and put their arms out, forming a "net" to catch the trapped fire victim. (Make sure everyone removes watches and other jewelry that could scratch. It would be ironic to "save" someone from an imaginary fire only to have him or her injured with real cuts!)

Everyone holds out their arms with palms up, alternating arms with the person across from them. (Note: if they hold on to each other's hands it creates very high stress on the wrists when the leaper lands.)

Perhaps it is best to tell people to choose which height they want to jump from, but start low – maybe even at ground level – if anyone is frightened. Later, when we feel more confident, we can leap from higher levels, though I'd stop at about six feet (just under 2 meters). Now we're almost ready.

Make sure that all the people in the lines have their heads back, out of the way. Insist that jumpers have their arms out in front of them, thereby protecting their faces and spreading their weight over more people. Jumpers should also remove their shoes, especially if hard. Now, when ready, jump! After you have demonstrated the leap yourself (yes, you), have the next person stand at a distance from the end facing the lines.

It is very important to make sure that all the safety precautions are followed and that everyone is paying attention. The first time I presented this game with my co-worker, Jan Spector, in San Francisco, I didn't fully take notice that there were two small boys opposite each other where Jan's head would land. But everyone noticed when she fell through their arms and nearly broke her nose.

Though it can be scary (*I* always hesitate), when you jump and land it feels great. It's nowhere near as bad as it looks. And the leaper is saved from the fire. (Where's the fire? Oh, yes, that's where we started this game.)

Games for Your Backyard (Many Players)

~ Cat and Mice (5 – 50 players) ~

One day you find that mice have invaded your house, and though they're cute little fellows, you want them to go away. For those of you who couldn't kill a mosquito (and that takes *real* love for all God's creatures), there is a peaceful, nay, spiritual solution: transformation.

First, we get a cat. (I know what you're thinking, but wait!) All the mice are on one side of the "room." When the cat says, "go," all the mice race to the other side of the room trying to avoid the cat. However, the inevitable happens, and our cat catches a mouse to whom he does no more than tag. One thing I didn't tell you was that this is a magical cat.

The mouse then undergoes a change not visible in his body, but only through his behavior: He becomes a "mousetrap." He starts catching and holding other mice until the cat can transform them into a mousetrap, too. By the end, all the mice have been changed into mousetraps! Since

some mice have a little more energy and some traps a little more strength than others, remind everyone that while mice can escape if they can get out of the trap, both mouse and trap should try not to damage each other. A change in the way mice and mousetraps move may be required to ensure safety of both –to hopping, for instance – and it may be wise to ask everybody to remove jewelry, glasses, and anything that could scratch and harm another person, or get damaged as a result of playing this game.

(See, you thought there would be bloodshed, didn't you?)

~ Fire Engine (10 – 50 players) ~

Do you remember, as a child, seeing a fire engine hurtling down the street? Did you ever wish you could be on it? Now, you can! In fact, now you can *be* the Fire Engine.

Have the group divide into parallel lines of five or so people, all facing the same direction. Point out a "fire" that is at a location 15 or more yards away. Each of us, as fire engines, must try to put it out. Since it doesn't look like too big a fire at this point, each line at first only sends one engine (person), with siren wailing European-style, "wee-woo, wee-woo, wee-woo!", and lights flashing (that is, one arm flapping in a circle above her head).

Upon arrival, the engines take their fire hoses and spray the fire. Each engine discovers that they need help, so they go back ("wee-woo, wee-woo…") to get another engine. This is repeated, because it turns out to be a big fire getting bigger still, until each line gets all its engines to the scene of the blaze. In Stockholm, men and women in normal business dress played this game, which was quite a sight to behold. Any real fireman would certainly have laughed himself silly watching the spectacle.

~ Robots (10 – 50 players) ~

You now can have your very own robot – in fact, you can have two! Have everybody get into groups of three – a couple of fours are fine, if the number of people makes it necessary. One person must act as the human robot controller who starts up and guides her robots. The robots may only go in a straight line until their direction is changed by the controller.

If a robot should run into an obstacle such as the designated boundary, or another robot, it stops and needs to send out an SOS signal such as "Beep-beep-beep…" until the robot controller redirects the troubled android. Before starting, the robots and controllers can agree on their own unique warning signal to help distinguish them from other robots.

After a minute, have robots and controller get together again and pick a new controller, and then again, after another few minutes, to give everyone a chance to be controller. Immediately after this game, I doubt if you'll find many people amongst yourselves who will support automation.

~ Wizards (5 – 50 players) ~

Since play is magical (after all, you were just introduced to a magical cat a few games back), it's time you were introduced to the Wizards. Our magic makers seek to freeze people, but only because they know that other people can unfreeze the frozen with a warm hug.

Have all the players form a circle and close their eyes. Go around and run your hand gently down the middle of the back of those who will become Wizards, with about one Wizard for every five players. Have everyone open their eyes and run to escape the Wizards. The Wizards make the same stroking motion down a person's back to freeze him or her.

No one knows who the Wizards are at first, even other Wizards, but we soon find out once they start freezing everyone. Of course, everyone is busy hugging frozen players to unfreeze them, making the work of the Wizards even harder.

In all fairness, and because Wizards like a hug now and again, too, after a few minutes have non-Wizards close their eyes again. (You don't even need a circle! Can you believe it!)? All the Wizards from the most recent round each pick another player to become a new Wizard to replace him, with the same backstroking motion. Perhaps you wouldn't classify this game as true magic, but a hug *has* been known to work wonders!

How to Lead Games

They say the seeds of what we will do are in all of us, but it always seemed to me that in those who make jokes in life the seeds are covered with better soil and with a higher grade of manure.

Ernest Hemingway

He who can, does. He who cannot, teaches.

George Bernard Shaw

Although people in my workshops have thought of 100 or more valid qualities necessary for leading games, I present here merely a handful of what I feel are the most essential ones. Some overlap each other. Most are common sense or at least appear to be, but all too often it's the light pole directly in front of our noses that we walk into, bumping our heads.

Safety Consciousness

The main thing that changes a non-participant into a safety-conscious player is the realization that the game is safe. A games leader, in order to create this safe atmosphere, is responsible for looking after both the physical and psychological safety of participants.

This can take **many forms.** For instance, before starting, whether indoors or out, the playing area needs to be looked over for potential dangers such as poles, low beams, table or other sharp edges, holes, glass, sprinkler heads, and animal traces (you know what I'm talking about) which need to be covered, moved or avoided where possible. Once people start playing, they seem to forget they can hurt themselves. For this reason, **players should be given a warning about these pitfalls before the session begins** with an occasional reminder when appropriate.

The way a game is presented will help determine whether it becomes a game of rugby (or worse) or a game everyone can enjoy safely. The dangers of very physical games can be demonstrated by dramatically exaggerating caution or using mock violence humorously, thereby raising the players' awareness of what they are doing to themselves and others. The general rule is, and this can be stated directly to players: **Don't play so hard that you hurt someone. Use minimum force necessary.** Having just written the preceding sentence, the games sound like they're pretty rough. In practice, they almost always are not, especially if you, as a games leader, create a friendly, cooperative atmosphere.

When a game starts to get too rough, we can either stop the game to remind everyone we're here to have fun and not hurt each other and ourselves, or say something like, "This game is getting a bit rough. How can we change this game so that nobody gets hurt?" This refocuses the group on safety. It gives everyone a share of the responsibility for keeping the game safe and also calls on his or her collective imagination to come up with a solution. The group will be more likely to respect a solution they themselves come up with. Pointing out a few individuals who are playing too rough tends to alienate them, and it gives them no chance to recognize and creatively alter their behavior. Handicaps can be created for players who continue to be over-enthusiastic.

While we always want to keep the game safe, there may be times when some players want to play more aggressively. Adults may want to play without their children and vice versa. As always with active games, it should be announced at the beginning what kind of game it's going to be, thereby making people fully aware that they can choose not to play. If this is not done, players are sometimes caught up in the spirit of the moment with realizing the danger to themselves.

Once you warn people, it becomes their conscious choice to play or not. For instance, at a play session in Govan, a tough section of Glasgow, Scotland, I gave the standard warning that we were about to do an active game and everyone should consider that before playing. The whole time I was speaking I was looking directly at a four-foot, sixty-year-old lady. When I finished she immediately piped up, "Well, you better tell these other people, then!"

Although the discussion so far has been about physical safety, the same ideas also apply to **psychological safety.** If the players sense your concern for their well being, they will trust you and participate more readily. It helps, of course, with a shy or non-athletic crowd, to start with gentle, non-threatening games.

Additionally, I feel **it's very important for a games leader to play the game her/him self** – the players are more likely to trust you and respect your judgment. As a player your attention will be on the game, and you can literally feel if it's getting out of control. As a games leader you notice what is happening to others. While it's advisable to join in at the beginning, that does not mean you have to play every minute of every game. But showing a willingness to join in for a bit is important. A general rule is: **The larger the group, the more attention required from you.** Never hesitate to stop a game when you sense danger. A few times I've waited just a little too long and someone got hurt (though not seriously).

Psychological safety includes letting people know that while they are welcome to join, it's also all right if they choose not to. Besides, someone who is forced into playing usually becomes an energy drain. A teacher working alone with his/her class can offer students who don't want to participate a non-distracting alternative such as sitting and watching, exercise, or reading. Having said this, sometimes kids are just messing around about not participating and can be coaxed into joining in: "Come on, just try one game to see how you feel about it." Usually if they're just trying to act cool, particularly if there's a group that says that they don't want to join, they'll get beyond it because they're having fun. However, we can't always tell what's going on for an individual. Maybe they're having a tough time at home, or something else is going on for them.

Usually you can tell if there is something really going on with a person – in any case, if they insist they don't want to participate, it is better to err on the side of safety. Let the person opt out.

I consider disruptive behavior that destroys games to be a decision not to play. From experience, I've found that an effective way of dealing with this is to ask the offending player(s) to sit out for at least one game. It should be made clear that she/he is then welcome to rejoin but free to choose. This is a positive approach – the player is not punished so much as excluded for a time from a pleasurable activity he or she has not supported. Self-control is taught through this. (This approach is not usually appropriate for adults.)

To create an atmosphere of psychological safety, a play leader needs to establish order within chaos, setting limits without anger. This means a clear distinction must be made between the person and his/her behavior. A firm but gentle response is called for and the ability to determine the difference between destructive and creative disruption. How you respond to the disruption will often determine how this turns out. If you are able to take the energy that is being expressed and use it rather than resist it, you can make it creative. This takes practice and a creative imagination, and it can be a fun challenge.

When players are asked to close their eyes for a game, request a player or an observer to take care that no one walks into danger, and let participants know that they are being watched over. That way they feel more freedom to play.

If someone does appear hurt, any good feelings that have built up can quickly vanish. What you as a leader can do is to ask if there is someone who knows first aid (or who can look after the injured player) while you move everyone else away so that no one stands around staring at the one who is hurt. He/she might only have had the breath knocked out of him/her or twisted their ankle a bit, and could be somewhat embarrassed by the attention. Occasionally, a person will seek to get the group's attention by overplaying their injury, or even faking it. Having someone look after them will give them some attention, while moving the group away guarantees that the session will go on.

If the person isn't badly hurt, which is almost always the case, this gives them a chance to recover gracefully. For the rare injury that requires further attention, have at least one person stay with the injured while another person does whatever is required – gets ice, or telephones for a doctor or ambulance. However, in all my years of giving workshops, the doctor has never been needed. (I hope I didn't jinx myself by writing that!)

Your responsibility as games leader / presenter is to know beforehand where everything that might be needed is (ice, first aid kit), or have available somebody who has the required information. A few minutes of inquiry before the play session begins can save anxiety later for you, the injured party, and the group. If you are co-presenting games, work out between you what to do if someone is injured. Then if an injury happens, you can function smoothly as a team where each leader knows what to do. Meanwhile, the play session can continue with the other players giving a little more thought to safety!

Playfulness

A games leader embodies the spirit of the games he/she presents and plays. If you're having a good time, it'll be easier to convince others to let go and have fun, too. Choose games that you like – this makes it easier to be enthusiastic yourself. On the other hand, there have been times when I presented a game that I really didn't want to play but which I felt would be right for the situation. If I was correct, the positive response of the group swept me up in their enthusiasm. Be able to laugh at your mistakes – everyone else will, and you might as well laugh with them.

Amateur comedians (i.e., almost everyone) can have a field day using stories and jokes in explaining a game. Of course, a lively group will want to join the act, which is always more interesting, if challenging, and should be encouraged. For instance, one day I started a game of

"Elephant, Rabbit, Palm Tree" on a day when I happened to be wearing a green T-shirt, bright red sultan pants with little colored hearts on them, an orange baseball cap with a green propeller on top, red and yellow striped socks, and brilliant red shoes. Jan Spector pointed at me and said, "This is a palm tree." I dutifully hoisted up my arms overhead to demonstrate a "palm." At this point, one of the players responded, "Looks more like a Christmas tree!"

Empowering

When presenting a game, you may sometimes find that players want to change your game or present a game themselves. When this happens you tell them to cease immediately. Just joking. It's a good idea to keep in mind that it's "our" – not "my" – play session. I advise staying flexible and open to suggestions, except, of course, to ideas that are obviously physically or psychologically unsafe. You can suggest a less risky alternative. Even if the idea sounds dumb, it could be a lot of fun. (You might even be reading about it in a future book of mine.) If it isn't fun, that will become apparent. Then you can ask, "How can we change this game to make it more fun?" thereby inviting players to play with the game itself. I recommend that you change only one element of a game at a time, or it gets too confusing as to what the rules are.

Getting Attention

To start a game, it is essential to get and hold the attention of the players. The better focus you have, the more likely that the game will proceed smoothly and be more fun. There will be fewer questions and more involvement. You don't need to be a dictator to do this. For instance, rather than shouting, "Attention, everyone, attention!" you can ask everyone to form a circle, starting it yourself by taking two people by the hands and enlisting their aid to take the hand of others. That can be a game in itself. When the circle is formed, you have the group's attention.

In extreme conditions, extreme measures are called for, such as shouting nonsense and acting crazy while making weird body movements until everyone watches you. (In Israel, where often everyone talks at once, this was one time the only way to get attention.) Try different methods to find out what suits you and what works in a particular situation.

Clear and Concise

Players always appreciate directions that are clear and concise. People fall asleep (sometimes literally!) or leave if an explanation is too long or complicated, or kids can start to get restless and disruptive. Fuzzy descriptions lead to confusion, at least a million questions and make everyone wish they were somewhere else. This doesn't mean you should forget telling a story or making up fantasy tales for children, but it helps to be organized and usually brief.

Inviting

Always invite onlookers but don't insist that they join. An invitation lets them know they are welcome, even if they don't want to join. It never hurts to extend another invitation at the start of new games, as long as you don't harass people. Some people respond to coaxing, especially if they secretly want to join, and it presents more than one opportunity to easily change their minds.

I have never known of anyone who tried to disrupt or destroy a games session after having been asked to join. In a workshop in Strasbourg, France, a very political woman asked me what I'd do if fascists showed up at our play session. Without hesitation I responded, "I'd invite them to join us." She nearly flipped out. Calmly I explained that the fascists would likely not accept the invitation – they're too serious – but if they did, they would be changed in the process since these games are somewhere between democracy and anarchy. This, of course, assumes that they don't come with guns drawn.

I remember way back when some guys who looked like Hells Angels (at least it was a motorcycle gang of some sort) showed up at the third New Games Festival (we called them "Tournaments" in those days) in Golden Gate Park and stood looking menacing. We asked them to join. In disgust, they got on their bikes and left. Then there was a slightly drunken lady who approached us in Durban, South Africa, and asked in a voice that said she was looking for a fight, "Hey, can I join?" I'm sure she was fully expecting us to say no and was prepared to heap abuse on us, but I said, "Sure, you're over here," and proceeded to explain the game to her. While she was taken aback, she actually did join and played a few games before moving on. Her anger was completely diffused.

Dramatic

Facial expressions, alternating loud and soft speech, and doing mime all help hold players' interest. Telling a short story or creating a fantasy for a game can increase everyone's anticipation. How you introduce games depends on your style. Experiment. You've nothing to lose. Dare to try something that you ordinarily wouldn't do if it seems like fun to you and see if the other players like it.

Repertoire

When the players are tired, they require a quiet game. When they are restless, an active game is called for. Again, if you are playing yourself, you'll be in close touch with the group's needs. As a person presenting games, you need to know a variety of games with various activity levels to meet the requests of the players for a particular situation. If someone asks, "Do you know a game with animal noises that we can play?" it's special to the player(s) if you can respond to it. Having a list of games handy helps. After a while, as you learn more games, you will be able to think of a game or way to adapt one that you know to fit most situations.

Demonstrate

In my opinion, the second most important thing to do, after you've made a game safe, is to provide a very graphic demonstration of what happens in the game while you are explaining it. Most misunderstandings are cleared up when players can see what you are talking about acted out. Naturally, for someone who is a little unsure of him/herself it's much easier, not to mention support giving, to demonstrate a game with a partner who already knows the game. Where one person has the responsibility for presenting the game, the partner can give support by asking questions if there is something that got left out, thus leaving leadership with the person explaining the game. Co-presenting a game can work, too.

Also, it helps to arrange the players in the formation the game is played in before you start to explain the game. If the game is played while in a circle, get everyone in a circle first, which helps make the game clear. Be as concrete as possible. Verbal, and therefore abstract, explanations alone are generally unclear. People misinterpret what you say, which gives them a different mental picture of the game. When the game starts, be the first one to do what you're asking others to do, especially if they appear hesitant. (As you play the games, you'll learn which ones are most likely to bring this up with players.) This helps build up trust as well as providing a clear example to follow.

Conclusion

Now that I've carefully outlined how best to present the games, relax! I've seen people do practically everything "wrong" and the game has still gone well. Asked if they understood the game, the players said, "No, but

I had fun!" The main things to remember are caring about your fellow players and enjoying the games yourself. Your concern and enthusiasm are enough to make a games session successful if the group is at all open to the idea of play. Try it. You may be surprised at how well it goes.

The experience you gain from trying it is your guide for what to do in different situations. Making mistakes is perhaps the most effective way to learn with understanding. It forces you to stop and look at what happened. The British have a saying, "Failure is the pillar of success." You will be less likely to make mistakes if you accept that you will make some. I make them even though I've been leading games a long time. And, a little secret, it's even all right to repeat mistakes – it just means that eventually you'll learn the lesson for sure.

Name Games

If you're like me, you have a terrible time remembering a name, especially if you only hear it once. Presented here are six different ways to learn your fellow players' names and still keep playing. I would not recommend playing these games one after another but probably just a few of them during a two-hour play session. A different one can always be introduced at another time.

~ Name Echo (5 – 40 players) ~

What's the greatest thing since a quadraphonic 3-D movie starring you? Would you believe a whole group saying and acting out your name exactly as you want? Well, why not?!

First, arrange the group in a circle. Then explain that everyone will take a turn going around the circle in one direction saying his name while making any sound or movement that suits him at the moment. Of course, the presenter (you!) will start thereby providing a demonstration and setting the mood.

You might roar out your name, "R-r-robert!" while making ferocious lion-like motions. Or maybe you'd be timid like a kitten, "Rolf." Or a choo-choo train chugging along, "Rolf! Rolf! Rolf! Rolf! Rolf! Woo-Woo!" In any case whenever your five-seconds-or-less demonstration is over, everyone else simultaneously duplicates or echoes your sound and motion, driving you either to tears, laughter or madness. Or all at once.

Then it's the next person's turn in the circle: "Heidi," leaping "high" for "Hei" and descending low in a bow for "di," again followed by the echo. This goes on until everyone in the entire circle has had a turn. Ask everyone to try not to repeat any motion already done to make it more interesting. And it must be a movement that the group can do. (Forget the splits and flips!)

~ Name Ripple (5 – 30 players) ~

This games also involves a name and a motion, but not your own this time. After we know a few names, we can invent sounds and motions for other people.

Again, we begin with the presenter in the circle, but this time the presenter says someone else's name with a gesture, for instance, "Car-Car, la-la," while doing cancan kicks. One person at a time repeats the name and kick, going in a chosen direction like a wave until reaching the person whose name is "Carla." Carla does not repeat her name and gesture but immediately says someone else's name with a new gesture:

"Svveeeennn," opening her arms wide. The process repeats until the wave gets to Sven, who in turn names someone else with a new sound and motion.

Before starting, it would be good to go around and have everyone say their name quickly, particularly if the people do not know each other well. The game goes on until everyone has been named at least once. No fair using a name of someone not in the circle!

~ I Sit in the Grass With My Friend... ~
(10 – 30 players)

Imagine this scene: it's summer, it's warm and the sun is shining. You're outside in the country sitting in the grass with your friends. Suddenly you realize you've forgotten many of your friend's names. Here is a way to help you find them out again.

First, arrange everyone in a circle, with all players sitting on something that designates his place, such as a cushion, blanket, or shoe. (Chairs can be used when inside.) Leave one place open. The game starts with a race by having both people on either side of the open space trying to move into that space (for safety's sake, especially if a group is too rough or fragile, you can make this the first person who gets their hand on the chair gets to sit on it), the winner saying as she claims her new spot, "I sit," thus leaving free the place where she had previously sat. The person who had been sitting next to the winner now moves so that he's next to her again while saying, "in the grass," thus leaving his former place free.

This space is in turn filled by the third person in a row (who had been sitting next to the second person to move), who says as she sits "with my friend," and names someone in the circle. The person named gets up and moves to the open place, thereby leaving an open place behind them. This is the signal of the start of another short race between the two people sitting on both sides of the new open space. The winner starts the process over again with "I sit."

This is not only a great name game; it's also a lot of fun especially when someone does the wrong thing. Before the actual start, it's a good idea to go around the group once and have everyone give their name.

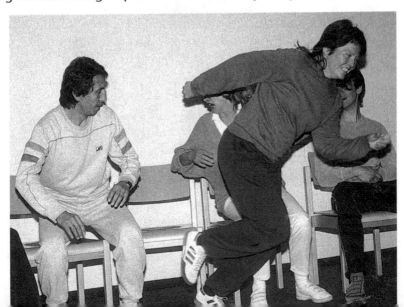

Let players know that if they don't know a name, they can learn it simply by pointing at a person while saying, "with my friend," and the person pointed at says his name as he moves to the open space. Once everyone gets the hang of the game, ask them to speed up. Not only will they learn each other's names, they'll have a better time remembering them!

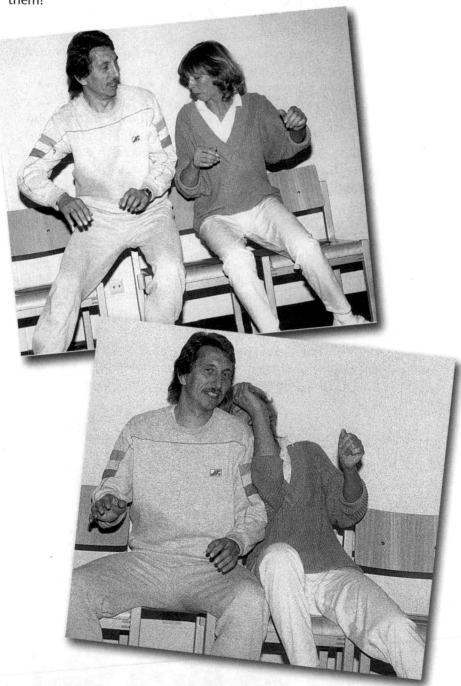

~ Choo-Choo (5 - 50 players) ~

If you've never been given a rousing cheer before in your life, this game is for you! It feels pretty good, that's for sure.

Once again, we start in a circle (surprise!). The presenter starts off by announcing that it's a name game called "Choo-Choo" and starts chugging across the circle by whatever path suits her fancy while making a "choo-choo" train sound.

Eventually she stops in front of someone and says, "Hi, I'm Annika. What's your name?" After the second person replies with his name (e.g., John), Annika breaks into a cheer, alternately raising an arm and leg on each side every time she shouts John's name: "John! John! John, John, John!"

Annika then turns around, places John's hands on her waist and they chug off together to find a new person to cheer and add to their train. After doing so, they turn around so that John becomes the new "engine," with Annika in the middle and the new person last – the cars in the train change direction each time so that everyone gets to be and engine and caboose once.

If the group is larger than ten people, we may want to split the train into at least two trains or more, depending on the size of the group, after getting four or so cars. This is not a game I would normally start a games session with, as it looks pretty silly and anyone who is apprehensive might flee. However, once the group has gotten into a playful mood, this game can really loosen them up.

~ Bumpity-Bump-Bump-Bump ~
(5 – 50 players)

At first most people have trouble saying the name of this game much less playing it, but with a few group practices everyone gets the general idea. Besides, it's fun listening to people try to say it as the game goes on.

Just for variety, let's start in an oval – most circles we make turn out to be ovals, anyway. The presenter stands in the middle and asks everyone to learn the name of the people on either side of him/her. Then, when the presenter points at someone and says either "left" or "right," the one pointed at must name the person on that side *before* the presenter finishes saying, "Bumpity-bump-bump-bump!" (The presenter should do this a few times so the group gets the idea.)

If he names the person correctly and in time, no problem. However, if he blows it by saying nothing, the wrong name, or even the right name too late, he takes the place of the person in the middle. After a little while, have everyone change places so that they are either standing next to someone they don't yet know or at least whom they were not standing next to previously. This makes it exciting for those who've learned their neighbors' names and gives them a chance to learn some new ones.

To stretch everyone's mind a little further, we can add the command "middle." When the person pointing says that, the one pointed at must name the pointer.

Also, we can increase the number of people in the middle to further increase the excitement, the number depending on the group size. (The maximum being no more than about one in the middle for every eight players.) The point of making any of the changes is that as players get better at the game, the one in the middle has a harder time finding someone making a mistake. So we make it harder for the players in the circle so that the person in the middle doesn't get stuck there while at the same time making the game more challenging and fun. Since this game is a bit anxiety producing, even though fun, I wouldn't normally do it as one of the first few games.

~ Doctor Memory (5 - 30 players) ~

Now to the true test of everyone's power of recall! After having had an adequate chance to learn each other's names (or not, if you're mean), we can ask people to recall everyone else's name from memory. Well, it's not *that* bad, actually.

First, arrange the group in a square or triangle (anything but a circle! I'm tired of circles. OK, but only if you insist) designating a "good memory" side. Or not. Then introduce yourself, "My name is Dale." Simple so far. Ask the person next to you to introduce herself plus you, "My name is Bridget and this is Dale." Each subsequent person must continue to introduce him or herself plus all those already introduced until the cir... (Oh, that's right, we're not in a circle, or are we?), square, triangle or other figure is completed.

Another version of Doctor Memory involves creating a new name using your name plus a word that starts with the same letter, rhymes or somehow fits with your name. A few examples, "Doctor Dale, Dale Whale*, Hill 'n' Dale." A variation of this is to ask the group to use positive adjectives to describe themselves, like "Dynamic Dale, Dancing Dale, Debonair Dale, Hale Dale." It's amazing how this silly association helps you remember someone's name.

In all fairness, the person who introduces and starts the game should also go last. (You'll be surprised at how you pay attention!)

When I was a child, kids teased me by calling me "Dale the whale," which I didn't like. Since the ecological movement began, however, whales have become quite fashionable!

Cooperative Games and Ideas for Making Teams and Choosing Partners

Back when I was in grammar school we always chose sides for team games. Of course, if you were chosen toward the end, or God forbid, last, you were seen as among the worst players. It was crushing to self-esteem. You also knew the other players would keep the action away from you as much as possible. For example, in baseball you would likely play right field (as I did) or more accurately, "left out." If the action accidentally did come your way, usually you were so tense about flubbing (or over-relaxed from disuse) that more than likely you would blow it. In the end, you lost the desire to play and quit, whether it happened at the age of six, sixteen, or sixty. Fear no more. Here are some playful ways to enter cooperative team play.

~ Cows and Ducks ~
(5 – 50 players)

Have everyone gather in close and ask which animals are their favorites. Depending on how many teams or groups you want to form, ask the group to reach an agreement and choose that number of animals. Try to get animals that make a good, identifiable sound. For this explanation, I'll use two animals, cows and ducks. Then have everyone look deep within (for about 2 seconds!) to determine whether they are a "cow" or a "duck."

Once they know, they are not to tell anyone. Everyone then closes their eyes and finds their own species by making the sound and movement of the animal they've chosen. As usual with eyes-closed games, make sure someone is watching that no one wanders into a wall or any other obstacle, and don't forget to announce that someone is watching over the herd and gaggle. The game ends when everyone has found their own species, naturally.

~ Huggie Bear (5 – 50 players) ~

First, we must learn the art of "mingling." To do this, we simply walk about and around each other saying "Mingle, mingle, mingle…" Next, the leader (and later, someone who's been designated) gives a command like "Huggie Bear, color of shirt!" Then everyone with the same color shirt or top gets together in a group and hugs. (Read on to the next game and at the end of this section for other suggestions.)

The game usually goes on for four or five mingles until we are ready to form groups or teams for the next game or activity. If you want an exact number in each group, say seven, your last command will be "Huggie Bear, groups of seven."

~ The Partner Game ~
(8 – 50 players)

You don't have a *partner?* What a pity! If you've ever had the dreaded experience of not being able to find a partner when one was needed, this game is for you.

There are a variety of easy ways to do this. One way is to ask everyone to get together who has a piece of clothing the same color as their own. It could be a sweater, skirt, pants, shirt, socks, shoes, or…? A similar way is to have everyone find someone who has a physical feature like themselves: same color of eyes, same type of hair, same height or same gender. We could also ask for the opposites of these, just to see what happens.

Then again, we can move into personal history and match up by: month or season of birth; first initial of your first or last name; birth place; city state, country, continent or planet (!) you are from (the last separates the men – and women – from the whatevers).

We can also get abstract. For instance, everyone is told at the count of three to hold out one, two, or three fingers – then find someone for a

partner who has the same number of fingers held up. Or ask everybody to hold up their left or right arm, and find someone who has done the same.

The possibilities are as endless ("How did you get here today? Find someone who got here the same way.") as your imagination – the few presented here are merely to get you started. Naturally, the same techniques can be used to make teams, thus eliminating the onus of being the last one chosen, or not being chosen at all. You might say these techniques are ways that take the worry out of being close.

Other suggestions (for forming random groups):

- Favorite sports teams (when you need two teams offer two choices, e.g., Cubs or White Sox)
- Favorite food
- Car preference
- Political preference (WARNING: This can be dangerous!)
- Have all players put their thumbs together pointing upward and then close their eyes. The leader, also with eyes closed, reaches in the middle and presses down half the thumbs. Players open their eyes and join the "pressed" or "unpressed" team. This can obviously also be used to choose one person to be "it," such as in tag.

How to Adapt Games

In the beginner's mind there are many possibilities, but in the expert's there are few. The mind of the beginner is needed ... It is the open mind, the attitude that includes both doubt and possibility, the ability to see things always as fresh and new. It is needed in all aspects of life.

Shunryu Suzuki

"What do I do if a game doesn't work?"

Adapting a game is fun and easy. Any game can be adapted to meet the needs of the group, space or situation. All you have to do is change some part of the game! It is advisable to make only one change at a time to avoid confusion and so that the effect of the transition can be clearly seen. You don't need to feel solely responsible for changing a game. The group generally has plenty of ideas. Your job is to keep the energy of the group focused while getting their ideas out in the open.

What can we change? Following is a list of some key elements of games with several examples and some new situations requiring possible changes for making the game fair and fun for everyone. The first possibility is to make no changes at all. Everybody simply does the best they can and that's good enough. Numerous possible changes are listed on the following pages.

Table for Changing Games

Sample Game	Example	New Situation	Possible Changes That Can Be Made
Ain't No Flies on Us	Played standing	Players in wheelchairs	Have standing people play in a crabwalk position
A-rum-sum-sum	Body motions	Players with limited mobility	Invent new motions that everyone can do.
Bear Hunt	Hearing required	Deaf players	Have someone also give the explanation in sign language.
Car Car	Players form pairs	Odd number of players	Make one couple a threesome and see what they can create.
Cat and Mice	Players aged 20–35	Active children (aged 5–10)	Simplify rules, extend boundaries and use more fantastic stories to introduce games.
Cat and Mice	Catching and holding players	A player who cannot be caught	Have all players hop, fast walk – anything to slow the action down.
Dead Lions	Played lying down	Players want too go in water	Instead of lying on the ground, all players must float – now they are "Dead Sea Lions".
Detective	Find-the-leader	Someone is unable to find the leader	Ask leader to change motions more often. Give detective more than three guesses. Let detective stand outside the circle. Add second detective.

Sample Game	Example	New Situation	Possible Changes That Can Be Made
Doctor Memory	Game involving no motor skills	Add throwing and catching	The person naming must throw a ball / other object to the person named, perhaps using only one hand.
Doctor Memory	Game involving no motor skills	Add throwing reaction	The person naming must throw to people at random.
Doctor Memory	Game involving no motor skills	As above, but increasing difficulty	The person naming must throw to people while everyone is moving around (small groups).
Energy	Athletically -inclined players	Non-athletic players	Start with games which require the least physical skill. Create handicaps for skilled players.
Fire Engine	Players aged 20–35	Teenagers join the game	Make game more active. Don't use games with too much touching, initially. Avoid introducing games with children's stories.
Friendly Football	Highly competitive game	Players who want to join in when the score is important	Add a ball or two. Place players in pairs, with an arm around waist or tied together at waist side by side, back to back, or at the legs or arms.

Sample Game	Example	New Situation	Possible Changes That Can Be Made
Friendly Football	Ball game	No one brought a ball	Improvise: could a Frisbee be used instead? Or a bundled up shirt or a soft shoe? Everything is potential equipment.
I Sit in the Grass…	Large, outdoor areas	Rocks, holes, sticks, glass etc.	Remove when possible. Move to a new location. Mark dangerous areas or make them out of bounds. If unable to do the above, warn people to proceed with extreme caution and slow the game down.
Ironing Board	All players are paired up	New players arrive	Have them form new twosomes or join existing partners to form threesomes. Split partners from old twosomes to pair with new players. Original players can explain the game.
La Ba Doo	Players have full use of their limbs	Players who do not have full use of their limbs	Require all players to restrict the use of their limbs. Only do movements that all can do.
Little Ernie	Repeated movements	Energetic children	Have the person named in the story run around all the lines. Have children hop or make two-legged jumps.

Sample Game	Example	New Situation	Possible Changes That Can Be Made
Robots	Sighted players	Blind players	Have sighted players play with eyes closed or wearing blindfolds. Small, slow steps.
The Partner Game	Players familiar with each other	Strangers	Use games that are guaranteed to mix people randomly.
Three's a Crowd	A tag game	Too many players	Make more 'its' as necessary. If the 'its' continually change, have them carry something which identifies them as 'it', such as a jacket or ball.
Trust Leap	Adult players, standing	Pre-school children	Require adults to play on their knees.
Wizards	Players aged 20–35	Elderly players	Contract boundaries. Make game less physically demanding (e.g. walking).
Wizards	Tag game	Player who can't catch anyone	Introduce a rule whereby the 'it' can change roles quickly – e.g. yelling 'switch' to reverse roles.
Wizards	Participation	Spectators who don't want to play	See if you can include them by asking if they would: 1. See that players stay within the boundaries. 2. Watch over small children.

Sample Game	Example	New Situation	Possible Changes That Can Be Made
Wizards	Game with few difficult motor skills	Add self-control, jumping and balance.	Have frozen players bend over at waist – unfrozen players must leapfrog over them.
Wizards	Game with few difficult motor skills	Build strength and lifting ability	Unfrozen players must lift up frozen mates to free them.
Zip, Zap, Pop!	Elimination game	Eliminated players still want to play	Have players change roles and stay in the game.

~ Last Couple Out (7 – 21 players) ~

A game that I often came across in Sweden was "Sista Paret Ut," or Last Couple Out. There were some features of the game that bothered me, thus making it a game to adapt.

In the game, everyone stands side by side holding hands with a partner forming two lines facing the same direction. The single caller stands in front also facing forward and yells "Last Couple Out!" The last couple in line then races forward toward the front of the line, one on either side (but a safe distance away from the caller). The couple attempt to reconnect anywhere in front of the line before the caller tags one of them. The runner becomes the new caller if tagged. The caller must wait, with eyes and head forward, until he spots one of the couple before moving.

Everything was fine until there was a caller who was too slow to catch anyone. In fact, it didn't take long for this to happen. This was tiring, embarrassing, and demoralizing for the caller. So I asked how we could change the game so that the caller would change regularly. One suggestion was that the caller can be "it" a maximum of five times. Not bad, but there was an implied sense of failure. Another suggestion was more fun. When a couple touched, all three players (including the caller) then raced back to the front of the line. A slow caller was generally closest thereby gaining an advantage, because the last one to arrive was the new caller.

Last Couple Out

~ Knots / Giant Knot ~
(10 – 50 players)

Two games that I often use, "Knots" and the "Lap Game," are easily adapted to meet a particular need.

"Knots" is a game where between six and ten players form a tight circle with their hands in the middle. They gently mix up their hands (perhaps with eyes closed) and, at a given signal, take two hands. If one takes the hand of the person next to him (too easy!) or both of another person's hands, they break and reconnect with someone else. Once proper connections are made, they are in a knot. The idea is to arrange themselves in a circle without letting go. Naturally, they are not required to break their wrists maintaining a tight grip. Hand contact is all that is necessary. For unsolvable knots, the group can break a grip and reconnect.

When there was a large group, I would make as many small circles as needed. This meant that I'd have to stay out of the game dashing back and forth starting the game over or introducing a new one to groups who finished quickly. A way to include everybody in the same game of "Knots" is by starting with everyone holding hands in a circle and gently making themselves into a "Giant Knot." Players keep going over and under arms and around people without letting go of hand contact until no one can move. Then, unwind back into a circle. Unlike the small knot, we know it's solvable since we began in a circle. Also, the presenter can participate (Hooray!).

~ The Lap Game (2 – 50 players) ~

Quite often I close game sessions with the "Lap Game," which visibly connects people, making them interdependent. To play, everybody stands in a circle close to each other and facing in. Then everyone turns 90 degrees in the same direction (all left or all right) so that they are facing their neighbor's back. Then everyone puts their hands on their neighbor's waist, being careful not to get too close or too far away. (A good way to judge this is that your upper arms should be at your sides while your lower arm extends to your neighbor's waist.) After a practice where you sit back to touch briefly to see if any adjustments are needed, you give the magic words of assistance: "On my knees, please." Then everybody sits, making sure their knees are together, guiding the person

in front of them to their knees while being guided by the person in back of them to his knees. Thus you have a seated circle. One is featured on the cover of this book.

Unfortunately, groups of people keep trying to establish the "World Record Lap Game." This appears contrary to the spirit of cooperative games mainly because it's deadly boring waiting while thousands of people get organized to accomplish this. Also, suppose you only have two people. Edith and Erri from Groningen, Holland, invented a variation that guarantees a tie of a record every time! "The World's Smallest Lap Game."

~ Elephant, Rabbit, Palm Tree ~
(10 – 30 players)

Finally, there is an imaginative variation of the game called "Elephant, Rabbit, Palm Tree." The game goes like this: The leader starts in the middle of the circle and points at someone and says either "elephant," "rabbit," or "palm tree." The person pointed at becomes the centerpiece (trunk for elephant, bunny paws up for rabbit, or palm branches – arms extended overhead), and the two adjacent people supply large ears for the elephant, tall ears for the rabbit, or side branches for the palm tree. After a few practices to get the idea, if somebody does the wrong thing, they take the place of the person in the middle.

Challenge can be added by:

- having the middle person count to five (and later to three, as everyone gets quicker), by which time the threesome must be ready (the leader can help count)

- after a while, including a "donkey," where motion is forbidden by the person pointed at as well as the person on either side

- having more than one person in the middle, who point to different people simultaneously.

A more involved and creative variation is to start by dividing the players into groups of as many roles as you want to create, though more than five gets confusing. It could be plants, animals, or situations – anything from ballet to bananas (but not you, Anna!). Then, have these groups present their creations. Have the whole group practice the creation of each group, and then play including these new additions. It's good to start with only a few roles, adding more as people get the hang of those already presented.

My friend Martin from Vienna had a crazy group in Saarbrueken, Germany, that came up with things like "Fire Engine" with someone acting as a wild driver, someone else climbing a ladder, and the third person twirling an arm in the air for a flashing light while all made a siren wail. With self-entertainment like that, who needs television?

~ Friendly Football (8 – 24 players) ~

Football (soccer, in the U.S.) is probably the most well-known and popular sport in the world today. Usually it is played with people of similar ability. Although I've seen fathers play football with their sons, I have never seen mothers and daughters included (though this is starting to change). Again applying the rule that everyone wants to join if they only could, we can mess with the rules of the game to find a way that everyone can participate happily. One easy thing you can do is to attach two players by tying one player's right leg to his partner's left leg. You can use shoestrings if nothing else is available, as I once did at the Festival of Fools in Amsterdam.

Perhaps each adult could be attached to a child, or a woman to a man – some way that makes everyone equal. The level of competition declines quickly because no one is expert (unless they normally play that way, but I doubt it!) and the pace is considerably slower. It's impossible to take the game too seriously. If one side is clearly superior, swap a few pairs to even it out.

I *did* say NO equipment was required for any of these games. No problem. As mentioned under *Equipment* in the charts preceding this section, many things can be used. I saw players in Scotland using a tin can. No can? Use a paper cup. Or a plastic bag with something stuffed in it. Your imagination will help you find what you need.

> *He who laughs, lasts.*
> Attributed to Mary Pettibone Poole

Daughter: Daddy, are these serious conversations?
Father: Certainly they are.
D: They're not a sort of game that you play with me?
F: God forbid... but they are sort of a game that we play together.
D: Then they're not serious!

* * *

F: Suppose you tell me what you would understand by the words "serious" and a "game."
D: Well... if you're... I don't know.
F: If I am what?

D: I mean . . . the conversations are serious for me, but if you are only playing a game...

F: Steady now. Let's look at what is good and what is bad about "playing" and "games." First of all, I don't mind – not much – about winning or losing. When your questions put me in a tight spot, sure, I try a little harder to think straight and to say clearly what I mean. But I don't bluff and I don't set traps. There is no temptation to cheat.

D: That's just it. It's not serious to you. It's a game. People who cheat just don't know how to *play*. They treat a game as though it were serious.

F: But it is serious.

D: No it isn't – not for you it isn't.

F: Because I don't even want to cheat?

D: Yes – partly that.

F: But do you want me to cheat and bluff all the time?

D: No – of course not.

F: Well, then?

D: Oh – Daddy – you'll *never* understand.

F: I guess I never will.

F: Look, I scored a sort of debating point just now by forcing you to admit that you don't want to cheat – and then I tied on to that admission the conclusion that therefore the conversations are not "serious" for you either. Was that a sort of cheating?

D: Yes – sort of.

F: I agree – I think it was. I'm sorry.

D: You see, Daddy – if I cheated or wanted to cheat, that would mean that I was not serious about the things we talked about. It would mean that I was only playing a game with you.

F: Yes, that makes sense.

* * *

D: But it doesn't make sense, Daddy. It's an awful muddle.

F: Yes – a muddle – but still a sort of sense.

D: How, Daddy?

* * *

F: You brought up two questions. And really there are a lot more... We started from the question about these conversations – are they serious? Or are they a sort of game? And you felt hurt that I might be playing a game, while you were serious. It looks as though a conversation is a game if a person takes part in it with one set of emotions or ideas – but not a "game" if his ideas or emotions are different.

D: Yes, it's if your ideas about the conversation are different than mine…

F: If we *both* had the game idea, it would be all right?

D: Yes – of course.

F: Then it seems to be up to me to make clear what I mean by the game idea. I know that I am serious – whatever that means – about the things we talk about. We talk about ideas. And I know that I play with the ideas in order to understand them and fit them together. It's "play" in the same sense that a small child "plays" with blocks… .And a child with building blocks is mostly very serious about his "play."

D: But is it a *game*, Daddy? Do you play *against* me?

F: No. I think of it as you and I playing together against the building blocks – the ideas. Sometimes competing a bit – but competing as to who can get the next idea into place. And sometimes we attack each other's bit of building, or I will try to defend my built-up ideas from your criticism. But always in the end we are working together to build the ideas up so that they will stand.

Gregory Bateson

Life Is a New Game

Most people do not take playing seriously. On the one hand, that is exactly as it should be – playfulness and seriousness are opposites defining each other. However, this does not mean, as some "serious" people think, that play is superficial and has no real value. Seriously speaking, play is not *only* fun but deepens and stimulates creative thinking, especially when the player's imagination and ideas are integrated into the games. People get motivated to go past their limits. This creative energy can then be used to solve problems both on a personal and professional level. (If you haven't read the quote by Gregory Bateson about "play" and "seriousness" that precedes this section, I suggest you do so now to get a perspective on this.)

New Games themselves represent only one aspect of the life-as-a-game philosophy, but the idea behind them extends into all areas of living. For example, there are other worthwhile goals besides merely winning, like participating. For the vast majority of people left out of traditional sport and recreation programs, just being able to play New Games is a meaningful "victory." Another use of New Games is at work, where a relaxed, playful atmosphere helps build team spirit. This team building ultimately means more and better work done. Also, mundane tasks such as housework can be given new playful dimensions. Finally, I feel that play has a transformative potential for healing and growth.

What happens to people when they play New Games is nothing short of miraculous. One time while playing in a Stockholm park, I noticed an elderly Swedish gentleman observing us with interest from across the street. Then he came over to our side of the street for a closer look. At this point I invited him to join us. He smiled but shook his head, "No." The next time I looked he was even closer and again I asked him to participate. This time he laughed but once more refused. When I noticed him next, he had joined us playing!

Later, he came up and said, "When you first asked me to join, I said to myself, 'No, I'm too old.' When you asked the second time, I thought once again, 'I'm too old!' You see, I've been a businessman for forty years and in all that time I never played. But finally I realized, watching you play, 'I'm not too old!' and I joined in."

Meet Your Limitations: Special Populations

The idea of setting limitations for games works in two ways: (1) on the leader's expectations and (2) on the expectations of the participants. Once, when I was living in San Francisco, I was planning for my first play session with people from a senior citizens' center. I came up with about five games I thought they could do, about six more that I thought *maybe* they could do, and a whole lot more games that I knew that was *no way* they could do. I should mention that I had always been a bit squeamish around old people I didn't know – reflecting perhaps my own fear of growing old.

When they arrived, much to my dismay, I saw that some were in wheelchairs and others were missing a limb or two. Good lord! I had not counted on that. I had never had a group like this before. I thought, "What do I do with these people for two whole hours?" First we played the five "safe" games. No problems, but we were finished with those in twenty minutes. The six "maybe" games were completed in another twenty-five minutes. Now what to do?

The group seemed to be really enjoying themselves, so I thought, "What the heck, why not try some of the games I don't think they can do." After all, I *had* to do *something*. To my surprise, they automatically adjusted the games individually or made suggestions for everyone to follow so that they could all enjoy the game.

For a simple example, when we played "Cat and Mice," which calls for running, they simply each went at their own speed, which in some cases meant walking. It didn't seem to dampen their enthusiasm for the game. When one elderly man started wobbling and looked like even walking was too big a challenge, without a word being said someone went over and paired up with the man, giving him support. This showed me that the limitations were more in my own mind than theirs.

Playing at Work

New Games also has a role in the workplace. The games can be used simply for relaxation or as an energizer during a meeting or conference. Some New Games also have the potential to be used as tools on a deeper level to help solve problems by improving communication, bringing out creativity, and acting as a mirror of the work situation. The latter should be done with sensitivity and only after the group members have developed a trust in each other and in what we are doing together. At least a day is required to establish this trust and an ongoing commitment to maintain it.

For me, the problem solving and conflict resolution aspects are the most exciting areas of games playing. They are the basis for my latest "new games," which present a real challenge in that they have the potential to go much deeper than the other work I do. This can be done with a group after establishing a safe environment with New Games initially used just for fun. The games for the next step of problem solving and conflict resolution require absolute cooperation to work successfully.

Whatever happens during a game then becomes the subject matter for a reflective discussion examining our own role, that of others, and the group's interactions. This would not likely have been possible from the start, where we did the games for fun and without discussion, but having established an open atmosphere where ideas and opinions flow freely concerning our relations in a game setting, we can then switch over to the work setting to see if the same or different behavior occurs. Needless to say, this is a delicate process that demands sensitivity to make it work.

While in Adelaide, Australia, I played with the whole office staff at a Work Preparation Centre for job rehabilitation. At first the men were wearing suits and ties and, along with the women, had looks of doubt on their faces. Their boss was enthusiastic about what playing together could mean to them, but they clearly had not yet caught the play bug.

After one half hour of playing, though, the suits, ties, and odd looks were shed. The "boss" and lowest paid clerk were equals: Their ideas counted just the same. The business manager commented to me later, "We've never had so much fun together. I feel I know the others a bit better now because I got to see a side of them I have never seen before." Though our time together had been brief, it confirmed for me once again that New Games and more advanced play forms belong in the business world.

The Search for Alexander's Nose

However, not every business office can take time to play for a few hours, or even ten minutes, once a week. The New Games Foundation in San Francisco was a prime example. There we were, an organization dedicated to getting others to engage in cooperative play, and we had become so busy that we stopped playing ourselves! "We" had become "them." Like the famous *Pogo* cartoon had said, "We have met the enemy, and he is *us*."

What to do? Everybody claimed that they were overloaded with work, which was true (sound familiar?). At about the same time a national museum tour, "The Search for Alexander" was in San Francisco. The publicity poster for the show had a bust of Alexander the Great. However, the bust had been damaged, the nose was chipped off. This gave rise to a local joke that the exhibit should be called "The Search for Alexander's Nose." Then someone came into the New Games office wearing one of those Groucho Marx glasses with bushy eyebrows, moustache, *and* a big nose. Removing the nose from the disguise gave us all the elements we needed to invent a game that we could play in the office without significantly upsetting the work. And, yes, we called the game "The Search for Alexander's Nose."

The game is very simple. Someone would hide the "nose" somewhere in the office – everyone else would have to try to find it. The staff rarely ever searched for it, but eventually someone would come across it. Sometimes it would take ten minutes. Or it could take up to ten days. Hiding places such as among the coffee filters, in the filing cabinets, or in the light fixtures became too easy. Imaginations were truly stretched.

Whenever it was found, the discoverer would loudly proclaim something like, "So, *there's* Alexander's nose!" and everyone would come to see where it had been hidden. The finder then had to hide the nose again for the next round of play. The challenge was to find a place no one else had thought of before. All this took only a minute, but it provided a playful break at the most unexpected times and reminded the staff why they were working there in the first place.

It didn't take long to exhaust all the obvious locations and also to realize that this was a fun, ongoing game. If a machine jammed there was a good chance it was Alexander's nose. The nose was discovered one time taped to the underside of the toilet lid. The hiding places became more thoughtful and exotic as time went on. Eventually the boundaries of the office became too small for the game. One staff member went out for muffins and rolls and at the coffee break another staff member bit into Alexander's nose. The coffee shop had baked it into a muffin. Once the nose came in the morning mail with the return address of Alexandria, Virginia.

The game was so much fun we started using it as an example of play in the work setting during our trainings. One time we were doing a workshop in Plano, Texas, just outside Dallas, and told the trainees about the nose. People responded well and we got into elaborating about all the wild places the nose had turned up. One time someone had emptied out a small cream container and resealed it with the nose inside for the next unsuspecting coffee drinker.

At each workshop we held a public festival where the community was invited to participate in New Games. The trainees practiced their games leading skills in a true live test. During this open play session in Plano a stranger came around asking for Nancy Miller, my co-trainer. Upon being introduced he handed her a plain, brown paper bag explaining, "I believe this is yours," and left. Inside was, that's right, Alexander's nose. A staff member mailed the nose to a relative in Dallas with instructions to deliver it to Nancy.

After the festival when we discussed the experience of leading games Nancy had a great story to tell. When people realized that the very nose they had heard of had made it to their festival they were ecstatic. A standing ovation greeted the unbagging of the nose.

It's in Your Living Room!
Or, A "Clean" Game

This philosophy of play extends beyond New Games or even the workplace and into your home. Oh, yes! An example from my own life involves my former wife, Janka, who then taught computer science at Stockholm University, and me. The problem was that Janka hated to vacuum. At first I didn't mind taking care of it while she did other cleaning. After some months, however, I got a little bored with this routine. I wanted to share more of the housecleaning chores. Janka had unfortunately not developed any great love for vacuuming in the meantime.

At this point I suggested that we make a game out of cleaning house. At first Janka wasn't too keen if it meant she had to vacuum, but after a couple of tries, we hit on a game we both loved. It went like this: We would start as usual with me vacuuming and her cleaning the bathroom. The difference was that now we had taken the kitchen timer, set it for five minutes, and placed it halfway between where we were working.

When the timer went off, a race would ensue – whoever touched the timer first would get to choose if he/she wanted to change or continue what he/she was doing. The one who lost would get to set the timer for at least five minutes – or more, so as to catch the winner off guard. What happened was a mad dash every five to ten minutes, with each of us crashing into things on our way to the timer. By the time we both got there, we would usually fall all over each other and collapse in fits of laughter.

After the first few times, it no longer mattered who won. If one of us won several times in a row, we began to joyfully switch jobs anyway, to keep the loser from becoming discouraged. In all honesty, Janka never did become wildly (or even mildly) enthusiastic about vacuuming, but the memory of those times at least changed her attitude toward doing some of it. She smiled to think about those times, and that already was an improvement.

Player, Heal Thyself!

To state that New Games have a healing potential may sound far-fetched to most people. I know from my own experiences, however, that dramatic changes often take placed in people who play these games.

One time a man came to a New Games session directly from the American Embassy, where he had had a horrible day. He was upset and angry, and made it plain to me that he was sorry he had promised to join the games. ("Great," I thought, "So glad you could come.")

During the first game he managed a wry smile. By the next game the smile turned to a grin. By the third game, "Name Echo," where each person in turn presents their name while making a gesture and then has it echoed back to them by the group, he did a silly bow while affecting a British accent. When the group gave him his echo, he roared with laughter. Even after his awful day, the games gave him an opportunity to laugh at himself and restore his balance and sense of humor.

A more dramatic example occurred to me at the time my mother passed on. Two weeks after her memorial service in Chicago I returned to San Francisco. Even before I got into the house I was living in, I learned that it had been sold and everyone had to move. Then, later that week, a project I had been working on to take New Games into schools fell apart. At the end of the week I received notice that my unemployment benefits had been overpaid, and they proposed cutting them back to make up for it to twenty dollars per week. At this point, I laughed. After all, what else could happen?

After my second week back I was scheduled to present New Games at a day care center for psychotic patients in my neighborhood. When I arrived I was informed that one of the clients had jumped off the Golden Gate Bridge three days earlier. The clients were understandably upset. It occurred to me that we all were in a similar state of mind – I needed a break from my grief, too.

When it came time for me to lead games, I was introduced to the group. I stood up, but was unable to say or do anything. For the first time, I just didn't feel any energy to begin. After standing for what felt like five minutes, but was probably closer to thirty seconds, one of the male clients ventured to raise his voice and ask, "Hey, are we gonna have any games?" I looked at him and replied with all sincerity, "I hope so." His request was the spark that got me going.

We loosened up with a few games. Since it was a warm and sunny January day and we were right across the street from a beautiful park, I suggested we go outside. Everyone agreed. For the next few hours we played and laughed together, gradually forgetting all the heaviness that had been weighing us down. By the end, having gotten some distance from our fears and sorrows, we were ready to face the world again, lighthearted and refreshed.

"Where-do-we-go-from-here?"

As you may have gathered by now, I do not view play simply. The more I've played New Games and incorporated their philosophy into my own, the more I've found it could be applied to my work, personal, and spiritual life.

Not long after I started presenting New Games, I realized that the games are democratic in that everyone can play regardless of age, gender, size or ability. Specifically, this includes mentally and physically handicapped people, grandparents, children, prisoners, business people, anybody! And often at the same time. This has led me to be more accepting and tolerant of all kinds of people and their ideas. I no longer feel so judgmental – just as everyone can play New Games, everyone on Earth is part of the game of life.

The most interesting aspect for me currently is introducing New Games at the workplace. The games can be used for less weighty reasons, such as exercise, energizers, or relaxation. These are all valid. However, after bringing co-workers closer together they can participate in certain cooperative games and exercises which have proven highly successful for facilitating better communication, acting as a stimulus for creative new ideas, and, in a deeper sense, to resolve conflicts, though of course these have overlap.

Also, playful ideas can be practically incorporated into one's everyday life. Daily tasks can be transformed into memorable events and relationships can be improved. As Victor Borge, the Danish comedian / musician once said, "A laugh is the shortest distance between two people."

Another aspect of games and laughter is their power to heal attitudes and bodies as well. As he has well reported, Norman Cousins attributes the ridding of his collagen disease to greatly increasing his amount of laughter.

Well, where *do* we go from here? The New Games philosophy has metamorphosed my view of what is possible: I believe I can achieve anything that I really want, given enough time, effort, and spiritual guidance. The first step in making something happen is to *believe* it can happen.

Therefore, my goals are not modest in scope. I plan to take New Games to China and Russia as a means of personal diplomacy. Also, another exotic place I would like to present New Games is Antarctica, a place where good relations are crucial for survival. I also hope to become enlightened for myself but mostly for others, a goal that might seem incongruent with my other goals. However, I consider this the ultimate game and goal of my life.

Finally, I continue to use play, in the form of visualizations and meditation, to find out the truth of who I am and what I'm on Earth for. Other than being the deepest and most significant dimension of play (and existence), I've experienced it as by far the most challenging … and fun! That little three-letter word is vitally important in my life, for without it, living is like a series of boring classrooms.

It doesn't have to be that way. The key element for me is finding ways to make all the aspects of my life more fun. I don't just mean superficially. My goal is to be able to take whatever life gives me and be content, no matter what. Considering where I started – I remember being in a funk for months when I didn't get a grant one time – I've come a long way. Now when something bad happens, quite often I feel it at the moment and then move on. At times I am able to maintain the perspective of "And this, too, shall pass." Still, I have a long way yet to go.

Where and When You Can Play

Occasionally during my workshops someone will comment, "These games are great, but they would never work with my group." First of all, never say "never." Beyond that, if you say and believe the games won't work, it is probable that they won't. However, after being told this, I've gone to the groups who would "never" enjoy these games to help co-present them and, guess what, I cannot think of a single time that the group didn't like the games. Most often they were quite enthusiastic. It's hard to reject a chance to have fun. If you are presenting the games, it makes a big difference if you believe they can be successful.

It might help to prepare your group by first announcing that New Games will be presented at a specific date and time. Those who show up will be at least curious and it gives those who are uninterested a chance to avoid the situation. Then again, surprise might be the best tactic. Many who might think they aren't interested find that, in fact, they are. Very few people, unless they're in a real funky mood, are totally against playing. Skeptics often become the biggest enthusiasts.

...Scholars have been unable to study (the) "spirit of play," because they fell back on the obvious structural distinction and looked at games instead of at the experience of playfulness. Playfulness, or flow, is not limited by the form of the activity, although it is affected by it... People can turn any situation into a flow activity ... a way of life based on play could be just as normal, or fulfilling, as one based on work and achievement.

Mihaly Csikzentmihalyi

... working because you want to is the best sort of play.

Robert Heinlein

Of course, the "real" world is not a series of scheduled play sessions intermingled with other matters. However, it doesn't hurt to think of ways to integrate play and games into your everyday life. You might suggest doing a game or two before a business meeting to help relax and energize participants. See if you notice a difference in the quality of the meeting.

Or perhaps you can offer a change of pace at a party that's dull, dull, dull! Most students love it when a teacher offers a lesson in the form of a cooperative game – and, more importantly, they remember what they were taught. Exercises for physical fitness, occupational therapy, and motor and perceptual skill development are particularly easy to make into game form.

I even remember a San Francisco to New York bus trip that was livened up when the riders asked me to do some games with them in an Ohio restaurant parking lot. Everyone but the restaurant owner was pleased. Now I know we should have invited him to join, which might have at least started a friendly and perhaps playful conversation.

As we got on the bus and it rolled away, our spirits weren't dampened – we continued to play on the bus. This was made a little easier since this was the "Grey Rabbit," an alternative bus, and there were only two seats in front, the rest of the space was filled with covered foam pads. We

played some of the most active games I know, like "Cat and Mice" and "Wizards." There were some adaptations, naturally – we were all on our knees, to start with. I must admit that I was surprised how well it went, given our space limitations.

Then, there is always the question that was typified by the woman interviewer from a newspaper in Johannesburg, South Africa: "Besides being fun and including everyone, what's the purpose of these games?" My response, after a short shocked delay was, "You're really asking that?" Some people have trouble seeing the forest because of all those blasted trees. After all, how many activities of any kind do we have that are truly fun and interesting and open to ALL people in a safe environment? Somehow, I have the illusion that this is enough.

Having said that, there are numerous valid secondary purposes for the games. For organizations there's team building, conflict resolution, or improving communication. For teachers there's teaching listening and following direction skills. For schools and groups there are the developmental skills such as cooperation, trust, and problem solving, to name a few. The games also involve individual behavior like self control, creativity, and spontaneity, and motor skills like running. There are a lot more skills that are enhanced and improved by playing these games, and these are listed in the chapter titled *Developmental Skills*. But that's not the point of the games.

People are always looking for some reason behind everything. Actually, to borrow from an animated cartoon called *The Point*, the games don't have to have a point to have a point. You might say that the concept of these games goes UNDER people's heads: it's right there, under their noses! People in the Western world have a tendency to over-intellectualize everything. When people truly experience their own spirit of playfulness in any activity it is a moment to treasure – for that moment. Perhaps Csikzentmihalyi (a free taco to anyone who pronounces this name right on the first try!) in his book *Beyond Boredom and Anxiety,* says it best:

> People who enjoy what they're doing enter a state of "flow": they concentrate their attention on a limited stimulus field, forget personal problems, lose their sense of time and of themselves, feel competent and in control, and have a sense of harmony and union with their surroundings. To the extent that these elements of experience are present, a person enjoys what he or she is doing and ceases to worry about whether the activity will be productive and whether it will be rewarded.

Still, you don't need games or a group to play. Csikzentmihalyi goes on to say:

> Conversely, a "flow activity" is an activity that makes flow experiences possible. Such an activity provides opportunities for action which match a person's skill, limits the perceptual field, excludes irrelevant stimuli, contains clear goals and adequate means for reaching them, and gives clear and consistent feedback to the actor ... The concept of flow makes it possible to see work, and cultural definitions of life style in general, as much more flexible than they are usually thought to be. It allows us to question the necessity of drudgery and anxiety, and it suggests ways in which everyday life can be made more free. There is no reason to believe any longer that only irrelevant "play" can be enjoyed, while the serious business of life must be borne as a burdensome cross. Once we realize that the boundaries between work and play are artificial, we can take matters in hand and begin the difficult task of making our life more livable.

> If we continue to ignore what makes us happy, what makes our life enjoyable, we shall actively help perpetuate the dehumanizing forces which are gaining momentum day by day. Enjoyment is left out of the equations for production, rationalization, and behavior control, partly

because it has remained for so long a vague concept. Something that cannot be defined can safely be ignored. Instead of enjoyment, leisure is used as an indicator. Leisure, as defined in the various official documents that measure society's collective well-being (see, for instance, Executive Office of the President, 1973), reflects patterns of **consumption** *and has nothing to say about personal satisfaction. The number of outboard motors or snowmobiles owned, the quantity of tennis players or theatergoers, does not tell us anything about whether people enjoy their lives.*

If the trend toward increased mechanization of life is to be reversed – and social alienation and individual meaninglessness thereby reduced – the first step must be the recognition that there is such a thing as positive enjoyment.

Playing is an attitude which covers every aspect of life including the spiritual. The games presented here are offered as a method of reawakening your playful spirit, which is an aspect of your total spirit. It's up to you to use that rediscovered energy to make your life more flowing and experience it more fully. When you are playing, you're present in the moment here and now, your whole attention is taken up. There's no time for daydreaming or senseless worrying. Viewed this way, everything that happens to you is another element in the game of life.

Dorothy Maclean, one of the founders of the Findhorn Foundation in northern Scotland, gives us another outlook on playfulness. She relates a message she has received from *devas* (a word from Sanskrit meaning "angels"):

(Devas) present to you most of all a sense of humor, which can operate on all levels at once, which bounces through the universe with the speed of light. Being light itself, it melts and lifts all it contacts. The devas of fun have immense scope, with entry where all else fails. They affect all kingdoms, but in humanity they find fullest range.

It is the greatest privilege to be a deva of this attribute, to see the most dense darkness become light in a flash and open a pathway for myriads of our hosts. From the depths of despair, a smile can appear and a soul feel alive again, ready for change and movement. Time and place become nothing. There are no tortuous roads to climb, for an instant touch of humor transports a soul into another world, a bright hopeful world where anything is possible.

We do not tell you what to do; we are not trying to teach you. We are merely explaining, from our point of view, the wondrous work of fun.

God had created all wonders, but perhaps the most magic one of all is when, from the most unexpected place, we see a sudden blaze of light – someone has laughed, and all is well. Negative humans can switch in a second, smile, and see a way again. Those who are stuck in routine, those who draw to themselves all kinds of obstacles, can suddenly see the ridiculous side of life and thereby be freed.

Now, this… comes from His Holiness the Dalai Lama. *If we look closely, we can see there are two kinds of happiness. One is based on physical comfort. You can say, the happiness that's based on pleasure, or the happiness of the senses. Whereas the other kind of happiness is based or founded on the deeper mental contentment. You can say, one is very expensive, and often unsatisfying, the first one. The second one is not only inexpensive, it completely satisfies you.*

Sogyal Rinpoche

Riches come not from an abundance of worldly goods, but from a contented mind.

Mohammed

Contentment is the natural wealth. The luxury is the artificial poverty.

Socrates

Be content with such things as you have.

The Bible

My crown is in my heart, not on my head. Not decked with diamonds or Indian stones, not to be seen, my crown is called content.

William Shakespeare

For I have learned that whatever state I am therein, to be content.

Philippians, The Bible

There is no treasure like contentment.

Nagarjuna, Indian master

What is Happiness?

Happiness, when I was a kid, was playing. Playing with mom's pots and pans making them into cities inhabited by crayon and playing card "people." Or meeting up with neighbor kids or my cousins and jumping around in the hay in the barn. Everything was a game except when an adult got mad at me / us for doing something they didn't like, or I / we got hurt. Everything was new and endlessly interesting. Of course, growing up, that changed. I became, like most of my peers, analytical, logical and, well, boring at times.

Happiness became defined in how well I did at games, achievements, and various competitions – in team sports, board games with friends, or getting the good grades. Winning or doing well was being happy, for a moment. Losing wasn't and lasted a long time. It seemed I was headed for a life of boring tedium. But, alas, such was not to be. I didn't follow the script.

I dropped out of college for a while, since I didn't really know what I was doing there and had a look around, working in an inner city ghetto in Baltimore. For the first time in my life, I was in the minority, since all my neighbors were of color. I had a sobering awakening – feeling a bit of what it's like to be a minority, and to realize that though I wasn't sure why I was in school, I had an opportunity that the kids I was working with would not get. Since this door was open to me, I went through it.

Still, I felt some of my courses were a complete waste of time. Others, though, like the speech class and the introduction to art class, opened up new worlds for me. That did make me happier, at least momentarily. Somewhere during my graduate days in New York, I met some pretty goofy people who loved to play. As adults, we weren't supposed to act silly, but these people did, and it was fun. Like playing bumper cars with shopping trolleys in the supermarket. I kept trying to fit in to the straight world, but kept tripping over myself. Thank goodness. As one job would end (usually under the threat of being fired), I would look for another I liked better, that I enjoyed more. Until finding New Games. Now there was a gem. Still, I always thought I'd move on in a few years, but years became decades and, here I am, *still* doing New Games. Maybe it isn't a phase after all.

But, why are these games still fun for me; how do they make me happy? When it's at its best, I'm just playing and not thinking about anything else. I'm not worried about the rent, relationships, or anything. I'm totally present in the moment. If I'm not mistaken, this is one of the goals of meditation. It can be achieved in many other ways as well, of course. Dancing, singing, being in love and doing work you love can all be the source of being in the moment. Also, one of the elements that I enjoy most from the games is seeing others enjoy the games. After playing these games innumerable times, they don't necessarily make me happy in themselves, but when I see the reaction of other people playing the games and having a liberating experience, it makes me feel good, happy, and allows me to get into the spirit of play.

But these are still just temporary experiences of happiness, though not insignificant. It is good to know what happiness feels like. What about lasting happiness? Where does one find that? The temporary experiences I've described do give a feeling and hint of a more permanent happiness, but they end. Happiness that transcends all circumstances, whatever is happening, is the true happiness. The lasting happiness, I maintain in my search for it, is the path of spiritual discovery – the knowledge of your own spirit. This is the ultimate game, the grandest of play.

Various religions call it by different names: the soul, spirit, nature of mind or something else. Any other experiences of the spirit are temporary. While they do give a brief glimpse or understanding of the spirit, they do not give the long lasting happiness that, I believe, we all seek, whether we know it or not. So even when things go wrong or something bad happens, when you have found lasting happiness, (or your soul, spirit, or whatever you want to name it), you are at peace, you take it in your stride, you are able to transcend the momentary incident.

The Dalai Lama says, "The principle characteristic of a genuine happiness is inner peace." You are aware that there is more to existence than what's happening in the moment in the physical world. I'm not there yet, I'm a work in progress, but that's where I intend to be going.

Sogyal Rinpoche says that to find this inner peace and contentment, we can find it in two ways. The first is to work on our attitudes, to be satisfied with whatever we have and appreciate it. In the West we seem to think happiness is related to fame and fortune, but people who have that are rarely happy. More often, they are worried about losing their fame and fortune. Simply being happy with clothes, food, and a roof over our head is all we really need. That doesn't mean we can't have "things," but not to focus on them as the source of our happiness, because it doesn't work. Not in the long run.

The other way that Sogyal recommends is " to cultivate actions that support inner peace and contentment." The prime example he gives is the "skillful means of meditation, which gives you greater power over your mind and your perceptions." Along with this is the "practice of compassion, which allows your mind to become more spacious," that is, expansive and broad in scope. The last thing that Rinpoche says you must do "is the realization of the nature of mind, ultimate nature, which brings about the realization of inherent nature, which frees you, liberates your mind and yourself." Those brought up in the West might view this as being aligned with your soul and knowing it deeply.

In my own life, I have been learning to recognize and accept that my wishes/prayers are answered to lead to my personal happiness. I remember one time during my first years with New Games that for twelve months I worked hard to get a grant for setting up a New Games project in schools. I did everything I needed to make it happen, and I was sure it would. As the time drew near for the decision about whether the project got funding, I was so sure that it would come to pass that I uncharacteristically told people it was going to happen. It became pretty hard to recognize that I am basically a shy person. I didn't get funded.

This threw me into a dark funk which lasted months. And it was all wasted energy: As that time had passed, instead came an invitation came to go to Scotland for three months on a grant, which was marvelous, and definitely fulfilled my wish to travel and spread New Games. Coming back, the New Games Foundation asked me to talk to a school that wanted to initiate an extensive New Games in their lunch time program, and I ended up doing that. Which was, by the way, the same that I was seeking to get the grant for. So, my funk was doubly unnecessary. All I needed was a bit of patience, and my wish/prayer would be answered. This has proven true for me time and again. Maybe it didn't happen in the way or time scale I was thinking, but nevertheless, it was answered.

I have learned that good energy and prayers I put out do come back to me or are responded to, though not always how I expected. Part of my learning is to let go of expectations. This helps me align with my reason for being, and that gives me lasting happiness. Now I'm beginning to work on the next part, sending happiness to others, even those I don't like.

So, the grandest game of all is finding the lasting happiness or our inner essence that is permanent and does not go away. That, I feel, is our mission in life. My fervent hope for you is that you find a way of discovering that part of yourself. What else is there to do in your life?

... if we have this inner peace and contentment, then even when we go through physical suffering, our mind can still be happy.

Happiness and suffering depend upon the mind. This explains how there are some people who can have every material advantage, but yet remain dissatisfied and discontent. While there are others who are always satisfied and content even amidst the most difficult circumstances. In fact when His Holiness the Dalai Lama was often asked by people, by the press, 'What is the art of happiness?'...I've often heard him say, 'Granted that external situations and circumstances do to a certain extent contribute to one's happiness and well-being, but ultimately, happiness and suffering depend on the mind.' That's to say, how the mind perceives the five senses.

Sogyal Rinpoche

If we have food, and roof over us, let that be enough.

The Book of Timothy, The Bible

Contentment is the most excellent of wealth.

The Buddha

The Newest Games

So far I have been writing about how the spirit of play applies to all aspects of life. For me, that spirit has now come alive in a new and most challenging way – through games that help me look within myself.

Some of these "games" have been around for thousands of years: tarot, astrology, and the I Ching. Some have developed more recently, in forms of modern psychology such as Gestalt, for instance. These games give me a chance to play with ideas about who I am and where I am heading. As such, I have found them to be some of the most exciting and rewarding games I have played.

As in playing any New Game, a person must be open and ready to risk feeling at least a little foolish in order to end up feeling a whole lot more alive. The difference in playing these newest games, however, is that they go much further than the games we've been playing so far. Games for developing inner awareness offer players the possibility of seeing themselves more clearly, in a safe context, without defenses.

While these games are the most challenging ones I've ever played, I can't remember ever feeling as liberated or having grown so much during play. I began to become aware of what was happening in my life and relationships, and why. For instance, it was actually through such play that I discovered that my fear of getting too close in a relationship was based on the rejection by my first love twenty years before! My pattern had been that whenever I would start opening my heart to a partner, I would start feeling attracted to other women. This effectively pushed my partner back, guaranteeing my "safety" – and also our unhappiness. Through playing games of self-discovery, I began seeing my unconscious patterns as they started and was able to take steps to consciously change my actions.

In presenting these next games, rather than commenting on them myself, those who created the games or exercises will introduce them to you.

(Note to readers: In this following quote, Jane Roberts is channeling the spirit called Seth.)

We are beginning to learn the creative joy of play. I believe, for example, that all creativity and consciousness is born in the quality of play, as opposed to work, in the quickened intuitional spontaneity that I see as a constant through all my own existences, and in the experiences of those I know.

I communicate with your dimension, for example, not by willing myself to your level of reality, but by imagining myself there. All of my deaths would have been adventures had I realized what I know now. On the one hand you take life too seriously, and on the other hand, you do not take playful existence seriously enough.

We enjoy a sense of play that is highly spontaneous, and yet I suppose you would call it responsible play. Certainly it is creative play. We play, for example, with the mobility of our consciousness, see how "far" one can send it. We are constantly surprised at the products of our own consciousness, of the dimensions of reality through which we can hopscotch. It might seem that we use our consciousness idly in such play, and yet again, the pathways we make continue to exist and can be used by others. We leave messages to any who come by, mental signposts.

We can be highly motivated therefore, and yet use and understand the creative use of play, both as a method of attaining our goals and purposes and as a surprising and creative endeavor in itself.

Seth/Jane Roberts

The Transformation Game®

Sometimes life is filled with blessings, insights, and a heart-felt sense of connection with people around us. Other times we stumble through a series of setbacks, accumulating pain, even falling into depression; and nothing we try seems to help us get out of it. Sometimes someone unexpectedly appreciates us or offers to serve us – or we reach out to help another. Sometimes miracles happen, pain is lifted, new directions open up, and the seemingly impossible occurs.

Just as life is filled with this rich variety of experience, so is the Transformation Game®, a fun and complex board game developed originally by Joy Drake and Kathy Tyler at the Findhorn Foundation. Since the first Game workshop was offered there in 1978, thousands of people have played the Game in its various forms. Many more have worked with the Angel® Cards, with over a million Angel decks sold to date.

The original version of the Game is an in-depth experience for five players facilitated by two trained guides. It is offered either as a three-day intensive or as a weeklong program. The Planetary Game involves 20 – 120 people in a life-sized format where players can engage creatively with collective issues and challenges in today's world. The Transformation Game® box is a distillation of the original workshop into a board game that can be played at varying levels of intensity either with or without a facilitator.

The Game offers a playful yet substantial way of understanding and gracefully transforming the way you play your life. It recreates in miniature the soul's journey through life providing a context where people can look at the kinds of experiences they create, and assess the value of their particular patterns and of their attitudes and responses to life. It highlights strengths, identifies blind spots and limitations, and brings fresh perspectives to current challenges.

In the Transformation Game® box version, you start by creating a focus to keep in mind as you roll the die and move along your life path. Before being 'born', you fill your 'Unconscious Envelope' with a set of cards that indicate the strengths, challenges and inner qualities that have a bearing on your purpose. You choose a guardian angel and then move along your life path, taking cards from the Unconscious and playing them on the physical, emotional, mental and spiritual levels. Some of the cards bring awareness, others bring pain – and you can use awareness to clear pain. You also have opportunities to exercise free will and intuition, to connect with angels, and to share appreciations and feedback.

Although players move their "personalities" from square to square at the throw of a die, they are not passive participants. Many of the squares and cards require players to exercise initiative and imagination, to share on a deeply personal level and to make their own choices and decisions. The game comes alive through sharing and interaction. It is up to the players to decide how deeply to participate, and to make what they choose of the experiences that come to them.

Whether at a simple decision or a major crossroads, The Transformation Game provides a doorway through which players can move to discover their own highest truths. In clear, concise and surprising ways it supports players in recognizing their true nature as resourceful and capable agents of personal and planetary change.

The original Game was developed by Joy Drake, who lived at the Findhorn Foundation for 14 years. "I wanted to recreate the Findhorn experience in a way that would allow people to learn the lessons and receive the insights that that environment provides without having to go and live there for three years," she says. "It was a way of distilling the essence of the educational process that happens as we begin to view the whole of life as a learning arena."

Many others were involved in developing and refining the Game. Principle among these was Kathy Tyler, who with Joy developed the commercially available Transformation box Game. But there were also many hours of playing with "Game devotees" on makeshift Game boards, intense brainstorming and feedback sessions, and long

philosophical discussions on the nature of pain, creativity, God, spirituality, the personality, wholeness, how the world works, and a variety of other topics.

There is now a network of expert Transformation Game facilitators in different parts of the world, trained in different versions of the Game. Several programs and products now make up the Game "family" and are available on-line and worldwide. A specialized version of the Game, Frameworks for Change, has been designed for use in organizational settings, while the Frameworks Coaching Process (FCP) and MentorSpirit cards provide quick and simple methods for improving inventiveness, effectiveness, and satisfaction in the workplace.

InnerLinks, a company formed to research and develop Transformation Game programs and products is based both in the USA, where Joy and Kathy now live in Asheville, North Carolina, and in the UK, at Findhorn, where Mary Inglis organizes trainings and workshops in Europe and elsewhere.

For information about programs at Findhorn, see the Foundation website: www.findhorn.org or email: innerlinks@findhorn.org

To select cards on-line and for information about trainings in the USA visit www.innerlinks.com or email info@innerlinks.com

Joy Drake and Mary Inglis

BuddhaWheel

A game of many lives, the non-competitive BuddhaWheel has been created by Emily Preece, a mother of two living in Totnes, England. Based on the Buddhist Wheel of Life it takes the players on a journey through their many lives as Animals, Hungry Ghosts, Demi-Gods ... and helps them to discover what they and their fellow gamers really love and hate during the time they spend expressing their own individually created Hell or God realms!

The Wheel of Life image, created by Buddha, was painted in monasteries, temples and caves. At a time when the spiritual pulse was beating at the master's feet, and when all who were able were scrambling for the source, this was Buddha's first real outreach project. Buddha must have sensed its creation was an investment in the spiritual future of all beings – and now the power of the image, through BuddhaWheel, opens the hearts of players of all ages.

Emily speaks of the way the Wheel of Life inspired her creation:

"As a Buddhist studying the image I wanted to crawl inside it and recreate a working Wheel to understand its structure and process."

BuddhaWheel, as a game, returns to the root of what a functioning being is – a stream of consciousness, moment of mind following moment of mind. In order to follow the path this creates in a living being, Emily had to source definitions of the types of mind and learn about the potentials of those minds – a set of teachings known as Lorig. In BuddhaWheel the players travel through the different realms picking up cards that represent these minds, transforming and working with them to create a path to enlightenment. The cards are extremely insightful and relate to everyday problems that arise. This helps to make the game relevant to everyday life and creates a great conversation starter.

A couple of examples...

*Non-**Attachment**:*

Having been slim in your youth, you start to fill out. You put aside the idea of extreme diets and surgical liposuction as you accept the changes in your body.

Resentment*:*

Angered by the superior delicious food that the Gods experience, you throw your inferior food at a passing God. He experiences it as a heavenly flower offering.

Miserliness*:*

You hide the biscuits from the children in the house, wanting to save them all for later when they have gone to bed.

Emily continues, "It seemed I was in the process of translating a scholarly, 'book orientated' system into a structure that would be fun and inspirational for anyone to engage with. This was exciting! As an optimist possessing a rather childlike faith I had often encountered people who were dragging themselves along the same path I was skipping along. "Should it be painful to travel on a Spiritual Path?" I had wondered, "Should blossoming be uncomfortable?" Having become a mother I was gaining more and more experience of learning through play. Couldn't these principles be applied to a path of Faith? Buddha's acknowledgment of all living beings in the Wheel of Life spoke to me as an acceptance of delusion and karma, of all states. The lotus seat of every Buddha pushing up from muddy beginnings."

While the game might seem complex at first BuddhaWheel is really quite simple to play. Since there are pictures on the cards and board that show where the next birth will take place a non-reader, while not able to read the entire card, will be able tell where his or her next birth will be, which gives them more independence in playing than most games. It is easy for players to come and go, so there is also no disruption in play if anyone wants to take a break.

Emily and her husband Steve Rogers embarked on a summer of testing and were inundated with enthusiasm, children inciting them to play, people discovering and rediscovering themselves, spiritual discussion and laughter. Each session was completely different as they shared BuddhaWheel with a wide range of people, people who are new to Buddhism, seasoned practitioners, those of different faiths, and people who just want to have fun. They played at festivals, in cafés, on retreats. As a non-competitive game people could play for as long or as short a time as they liked. Many games were saved for later play.

"The Wheel of Life has taken me on a journey, and continues to with BuddhaWheel," says Emily. "Channels of dharma communication are opened up between people who have great fun watching their character collect good and bad karmic actions on their journey towards Buddhahood. We've had kids of all ages playing it too. It seems to break down barriers, encouraging adults and children on all levels to learn from each other, and enables players to discuss what's important to them in life.

When people started to request their own copies of BuddhaWheel we began to publish the game. A whole new phase of challenges await us, as we ourselves engage with Buddha's original outreach project, his original impulse inciting direct and engaging answers to all those walking an individual path. Some players have bought it as a gift, others to play with their own families. Some to break down barriers between people, others to break down delusion on retreat."

On a more 'Down to Earth' level BuddhaWheel continues to encourage and develop communication skills in its players and in an age dominated by computer games the younger players are particularly enthusiastic. In it's educational aspect Steve and Emily have started leading successful workshops in schools, assisting teachers in their exploration of Buddhism.

"BuddhaWheel is a beautiful game and very well-designed." explains Rebecca Sachs Norris, Ph.D. of Merrimack College, "With this game my students learn essential aspects of Buddhism through play that evokes living Buddhism – a way of learning that gives them a feel for the tradition and an experience they will remember."

And is it so far away, this enlightenment? BuddhaWheel teaches us that all living beings are surrounded by rich material, which we can relate to in the moment of mind we dwell in right now. All we have to do is play with it! "Many BuddhaWheel Buddha's have arisen already, often re-entering the wheel immediately to liberate the remaining players – who knows what karma it will ripen in the future..."

Emily Rogers has been a practitioner and teacher of Buddhism for ten years. Find out more about BuddhaWheel and engage with a taster of the game and its beautiful board at www.buddhawheel.co.uk or e-mail Emily at emily@buddhawheel.co.uk

The Quest

*(Note to reader: the following is taken from the book
The Quest, published by O Books, 2005)*

Getting Started

"Surely there is more to life than this!" you might exclaim as you grapple with the ups and downs of life or when your hopes for an enduring sense of fulfillment are dashed again.

Sometimes people find that a gap opens up when long-sought material dreams do not bring contentment. Others find they are no longer satisfied with the spiritual beliefs and traditions with which they grew up and they search for a wider, more universal spirituality that draws on the wisdom of many faiths. Still others want to engage with the forms of spirituality that have sprung up in recent years but are bewildered by the variety. These are quests – examples of people feeling drawn to what *The Quest* calls "exploring your sense of soul".

As the turn of the century approached, the three co-creators of *The Quest* – the Quest Core Team – met and explored some of these questions ourselves. We had each been pursuing our spiritual life and inquiry for many years and had varied experience: community and political activity, teaching, professional experience in writing open learning courses, theatre and arts, and living in a spiritual community.

We gathered together a group of friends and colleagues for a weekend of sharing our stories and searching for a sense of soul. Next, we formed a small team of people who complemented our ideas, skills and experience and shared our commitment to writing material that might help others wrestle with similar questions. During team meetings and with others, we explored our spiritual life and the spiritual, cultural, and economic transitions that seem to be affecting people widely across the planet. We tried to identify what helped us find our way amid all this change. We listened also to our inner sense of what spirituality meant to us, and wondered how we might more effectively live in the world together.

The Quest is the result of this work and we hope it will provide a guide for your search. It is a framework of questions, activities, resources, and ideas that help you establish, or deepen, an inner life that is real and meaningful. It is neutral in that the activities and examples in The Quest point you toward your own answers rather than a particular set of beliefs or practices that might be advocated. Throughout The Quest exploring your sense of soul embraces your beliefs, valuing your experience of spirituality, and those things that bring purpose and vitality to your life. It helps you become clearer in knowing who you are and more in touch with your innermost fullness. You will also develop a practice of spiritual reflection to anchor and deepen your sense of soul.

The Quest is meant to be flexible so you have choice about how to use it:

- **As a book to read and work through,** on your own, with a partner, or by bringing together a group of friends
- **As daily meditation or reading** that prompts questioning and reflection
- **As an intuitive journey** that directs you
- **As a "toolbox"** for exploring ideas and experiences as your interest or need guides you
- **As a course for professional development** where spirituality is a current or emerging interest
- **As a friend and companion** you can turn to when needed

However you choose to use *The Quest,* we recommend you make time to do the activities as this is how you find and clarify your answers to the questions that *The Quest* asks. We suggest you keep a record of your thoughts, feelings, ideas, insights, and responses to the activities in *The Quest*. There is no set way to do this; some people like to write, others draw, keep mementoes and reminders, talk on tape, write a poem, write music, choreograph a dance ... choose any method that helps you and perhaps try to use different ones from time to time. When you return to your record, it helps you see what's changed, how you've developed, and in what way.

The Next Step

Many people worldwide are on a quest to discover a sense of soul that is authentic for them yet still honours and learns from diverse wisdom, traditions, and religions. It is a "Zeitgeist" or spirit of our time and *The Quest* signposts a way to explore this contemporary expression of spirituality. Thomas Berry (1988) wrote, 'It's all a question of story. We are in trouble now because we do not have a good story. We are in between stories. The old story, the account of how we fit into it, is no longer effective. Yet we have not learned the new story.'

Berry draws attention to this period of transition between old and new stories; such major changes are paradigm shifts. Paradigms are conceptual umbrellas that help you make sense of your experience; they frame the questions you ask and the kinds of answers that are acceptable. In writing *The Quest* we tried to identify what might help you find your way amid profound change and listen to your sense of what spirituality means today.

The purpose of *The Quest* is to help us each participate in creating a new story for humanity. To play your part, you need to be willing to explore yourself in many different ways. Time and time again, you will find *The Quest* asking you "What do you experience and know directly for yourself?" and "What do you make of this?" The emphasis is on the kind of knowing that builds on experience rather than abstract knowledge. So your research material is your life, relationships, interests, qualities, beliefs, passions, and difficulties.

Many people find their quest is enriched by sharing it with others. Religious communities have long recognized the need for community, a sangha of like-minded persons with whom to share fellowship, experience, and understanding. You might consider bringing a few friends together to follow *The Quest,* or advertise in your local library or community center to start a group; *The Quest* website has some ideas and suggestions on how to do so (www.thequest.org.uk). The idea of spiritual friendship and mentoring is gaining currency; you may find ways to develop it for yourself or you can consult *The Quest* website for links, ideas, and information.

There is no set time for working through *The Quest*. People who have already followed *The Quest* used the materials over a minimum of four to eight months. Many people spend much longer. You may also find that you return to it at different times and at different levels. But however long you spend and whatever your starting point, remember that now is the only moment to be open to all that is around and within you, and prepare to take your next step.

Joycelin Dawes, Janice Dolley and Ike Isaksen

Developmental Skills

If it has not been obvious before now, I'll state it plainly: the main point of these cooperative New Games is *not for training* of specific skills, as such. They are mainly *just for fun!* However, even at a casual glance, it is obvious that many skills and features are naturally involved, and whoever plays the games practices the skills by doing them. Improvement is bound to occur.

Let's say, for instance, that a teacher or physical education instructor has just given a test, exercise, or workout. Neither the teacher nor the students want anything too challenging to do at this point, but the instructor would like to present something that reinforces certain skills and use of imagination while being a lot of fun. New Games, sometimes with slight adaptation, are perfect!

The chart that follows is made solely of key elements according to the games' descriptions as given in this book. These are given a double "XX." Those games which contain these as secondary elements are indicated with a single "X." To repeat again, any game can be changed to include or accentuate certain specific elements, as long as it's still fun. Without fun, the game is just another boring exercise. Please refer to the section on *How to Adapt Games* for examples of how to do this, particularly the examples which relate to skills.

There are four areas of Developmental Skills represented in the games that we will consider here: Social Behavior, Individual Behavior, Physical Features and Basic Motor Skills. This system is based on the ideas in Gerhard Hecker's book, *Kompendium Didaktik Sport.*

Developmental Skills	Fruit basket	Friendly Football	Fire Engine	Fire/Trust Leap	Face pass	Energy	Elephant, Rabbit, palm	Doctor Memory	Detective	Dead Lions	Cow and Ducks	Choo-Choo	Cat and Mice	Car Wash	Car-Car	Captain Video	Bumpity-bump-bump	Blind Run	Bear Hunt	Ain't No Flies On Us	A Rum-Sum-Sum
Cooperation – working together for a common goal	X	X	X	XX		XX			XX		X	X	X	XX	X	X			XX	X	X
Trust – building a feeling of group safety				XX	XX			X			X	X	X	X	X	XX		X	XX	X	
Problem solving – finding one out of many possible solutions		X		XX	X	X	X	X	X	X	X										
Verbal contact – interaction with speech (includes listening skills)					XX			X	X		X	XX	XX	XX	XX		X			XX	X
Tactile contact – physical touching	X	XX	X	XX			X	X		X	X	X	X	XX	XX	XX	X	X	X	X	X
Adaptability – responsiveness to fit the actions and movements of others	X	XX	X	XX	X	X	X	X	X	X	X	X	XX	XX	X	X	X	X	XX	XX	X

Individual behaviour	A Rum-Sum-Sum	Ain't No Flies On Us	Bear Hunt	Blind Run	Bumpity-Bump-Bump	Captain Video	Car-Car	Car Wash	Cat and Mice	Choo-Choo	Cow and Ducks	Dead Lions	Detective	Doctor Memory	Elephant, Rabbit, Palm	Energy	Face Pass	Fire/Trust Leap	Fire Engine	Friendly Football	Fruit Basket
Self-control – ability to direct one's body, speech and mind	X		X	XX		X	XX	X	X	X	XX	XX	X	X	X	X	XX	XX	X	XX	X
Creativity – using one's ideas inventively						X	X	XX			X	XX	XX	X	X	X	X	X			
Spontaneity – impromptu action without special directions given					X		X				X	XX				XX					
Pantomime – expression through acting movements					XX		X		X					XX		XX		X			

Physical features

Game	Visual ability – observation and peripheral vision	Skillfulness and coordination – complex body movements	Reaction – quick physical response	Speed – quickness in running	Strength	Endurance
A Rum-Sum-Sum	X	XX				
Ain't No Flies On Us	X	XX	XX			
Bear Hunt		XX				
Blind Run		X				
Bumpity-bump-bump			XX			
Captain Video	XX	X	X	X		X
Car-Car	XX	X	X	X		X
Car Wash	X	X	XX	XX	XX	X
Cat and Mice		X	X			
Choo-Choo						
Cow and Ducks						
Dead Lions	XX	X				X
Detective	XX	X				
Doctor Memory	X	X				
Elephant, Rabbit, Palm	X		X			
Energy	XX	X	XX			
Face pass	XX	X			X	
Fire/Trust Leap		X	X	X		X
Fire Engine		X	X	X		X
Friendly Football	X	X	X	X		XX
Fruit Basket	XX	X	XX	XX		X

Basic Motor Skills	A Rum-Sum-Sum	Ain't No Flies On Us	Bear Hunt	Blind Run	Bumpity-Bump-Bump	Captain Video	Car-Car	Car Wash	Cat and Mice	Choo-Choo	Cow and Ducks	Dead Lions	Detective	Doctor Memory	Elephant, Rabbit, Palm	Energy	Face Pass	Fire/Trust Leap	Fire Engine	Friendly Football	Fruit Basket
Running			x						xx										xx	x	x
Jumping													x					x	x	x	
Balance			xx			x															
Climbing																					
Leaning on							x														
Crawling							x														

Developmental Skills	The Greeting Game	Huggie Bear	I Sit in the Grass	Ironing Board	Knots/Giant knots	La Ba Doo	The Lap Game	Last Couple Out	Little Ernie	Name Echo	Name Ripple	The Partner Game	Pyramids	Quack!	Robots	Three's a Crowd	Wizards	Zoom, zip, zap, pop!
Cooperation – working together for a common goal	X	X		XX	X	XX			X	X						X	X	X
Trust – building a feeling of group safety			X	X	X	XX							X				X	
Problem solving – finding one out of many possible solutions	X	X	X							X				X			XX	X
Verbal contact – interaction with speech (includes listening skills)		X	X	X	X	X			X	X			X	X	X			
Tactile contact – physical touching	XX	XX	XX	XX	XX	X						XX	X	X	X	XX		
Adaptability – responsiveness to fit the actions and movements of others	XX	X	X	X	X	X			X	XX				X	X	XX	X	X

Individual Behaviour	The Greeting Game	Huggie Bear	I Sit in the Grass	Ironing Board	Knots/Giant knots	La Ba Doo	The Lap Game	Last Couple Out	Little Ernie	Name Echo	Name Ripple	The Partner Game	Pyramids	Quack!	Robots	Three's a Crowd	Wizards	Zip, zap, pop!	Zoom
Self-control – ability to direct one's body, speech and mind			XX			X	XX	X	X	X				X		X	X	X	X
Creativity – using one's ideas inventively	XX				X			X	XX	XX					X			X	
Spontaneity – impromptu action without special directions given	XX			XX				X	XX	XX							X		
Pantomime – expression through acting movements	X							X	X	X									X

Physical Features	The Greeting Game	Huggie Bear	I Sit in the Grass	Ironing Board	Knots/Giant Knots	La Ba Doo	The Lap Game	Last Couple Out	Little Ernie	Name Echo	Name Ripple	The Partner Game	Pyramids	Quack!	Robots	Three's a Crowd	Wizards	Zip, Zap, Pop!	Zoom
Visual ability – observation and peripheral vision	x	x	x		x			x	x	x				x	x		xx		
Skillfulness and coordination – complex body movements	x	x	x		xx		x		x	x				x			x		
Reaction – quick physical response	x	xx					x	xx		x						xx	xx		x
Speed – quickness in running							xx	xx								xx	xx		
Strength	x																		
Endurance		x					x	x	x	x									

Basic Motor Skills	The Greeting Game	Huggie Bear	I Sit in the Grass	Ironing Board	Knots/Giant Knots	La Ba Doo	The Lap Game	Last Couple Out	Little Ernie	Name Echo	Name Ripple	The Partner Game	Pyramids	Quack!	Robots	Three's a Crowd	Wizards	Zip, zap, pop!	Zoom
Running								x	x							x	xx		
Jumping			x																
Balance					x	x	xx							xx					
Climbing	x				x	x						x	x						
Leaning on	x				x								x						
Crawling	xx																		

Resources

Dale N. Le Fevre and his colleagues can be reached at the address below to lead **New Games at festivals,** to present **New Games Leadership Seminars** and to work as **management consultants with businesses and organizations** through **Playworks,** the branch of New Games devoted to businesses in the areas of Team Building, Conflict Resolution, Improving Communication, and Stress Reduction. Also available are Dale's books, CD-ROM, videos, and DVDs. These are outlined briefly, though more information is available upon request. All can be found on the New Games website:

www.inewgames.com

New Games Leadership Seminars

For those who are interested in learning and leading New Games, you may either schedule a workshop for your organization or find out the current schedule of workshops that you may individually attend. Key areas touched upon are finding a balance between competition and cooperation, establishing the right atmosphere for play and finding ways for including everyone who wants to join. Other topics normally included are establishing and practicing leadership, learning to adapt games, and creating a New Game together. Typically, 30+ games will be taught in a 2-day workshop, 15+ in a one-day. The current workshop calendar can be found at:

www.inewgames.com/gamescalendar.htm

Playworks for Businesses

Play provides a good starting point for working together. It gets everyone relaxed while seeing each other in new ways, and it stimulates creativity at the same time as building trust and creating good feelings between colleagues. The team building process starts with simple games, but in workshops of a day or longer moves to activities that are fun and require cooperation to do successfully. Various processes are then used to explore the blocks that are inhibiting cohesive functioning, and getting beyond the issues that appear to be causing division between people. Thus, communication is opened up, paving the way for resolving conflicts and thereby reducing stress. A slightly more detailed explanation is offered at:

www.inewgames.com/playworks/index.htm

New Games Educational Materials: Books, Videos, CD-ROMS, and DVDs

These educational materials are designed to give you maximum support in introducing and maintaining New Games in your program. Books such as Best New Games, Parachute Games with DVD; the New Games CD-ROM; the videos, Skill Games, Cooperative Group Games; and the DVDs, Best of Cooperative Games DVD, The New Parachute Games DVD, and coming soon, Best of New Games DVD. All these materials and more are available to read about and purchase on the web site:

www.inewgames.com/newgamesproducts.htm

Contact

New Games
P.O. Box 1641
Mendocino, CA 95460 USA
Email: dale@inewgames.com
Web: www.inewgames.com

New Games
Dale Le Fevre
201 Lancing Road
Sheffield S2 4EW
UK

For further information about the **Transformation Game** in the USA, weekend **Transformation Game Workshops**, and **Angel Meditation Cards,** please visit:

www.innerlinks.com or email info@innerlinks.com

For information about programs at Findhorn, see the Foundation website:

www.findhorn.org or email: innerlinks@findhorn.org

For information about Sogyal Rinpoche, Buddhist retreats, or joining others who are practicing Buddhists, contact:

www.rigpa.org/

Recommended Reading

To Hear the Angels Sing by Dorothy Maclean, The Findhorn Foundation, 1980

Zen Mind, Beginners Mind by Shunryu Suzuki, John Weatherhill Inc., 1973

The Tibetan Book of Living and Dying by Sogyal Rinpoche, Rider and Co., 1995

Best New Games by Dale N. Le Fevre, Human Kinetics, 2001

Human Kinetics is a publisher that offers a fine selection of books covering all aspects of sport and play. Their website is:

www.humankinetics.com

About the Author

It is not necessary to be crazy to be a writer, but it's useful.

Anon.

Suffer fools gladly; they may be right.

Holbrook Jackson

Dale N. Le Fevre was born at his grandparents' rural farm north of Green Bay, Wisconsin. He grew up on his parents' farm there and in the suburbs of Chicago, later graduating from Valparaiso University with a B.S. in Marketing and Management. Though his succeeding education was living in New York's Greenwich Village, Dale also received an M.A. in Education from New York University.

After a year in Rhode Island as a student union director, Dale moved to San Francisco in 1975 to become the main organizer of the Third New Games Festival held in Golden Gate Park, the first time this was done in an urban setting. In his two years working full time with the New Games Foundation, he served as office manager, associate director, and workshop leader. Dale continued to work as a trainer for the Foundation for several years.

In the autumn of 1976, Dale formed his own project, Play Express, to take New Games into schools. His international travels teaching New Games started in 1977 when he gave a course at the Open University in Britain. Since then, he has given workshops or presentations in thirty-two countries (at present), including every major country in Western Europe. Of special note were introducing New Games to Catholics and Protestants in Northern Ireland during the conflict there; mixed races in South Africa during apartheid; Muslims and Hindus in India; Jews and Arabs in Israel; church congregations in (then East) Germany; and Muslims, Croats, and Serbs in Croatia and Serbia just following the war. Dale has also worked in Japan, Australia, and New Zealand.

This, a revised version of Dale's first book of New Games, originally titled *Playing for the Fun of It* and later *New Games for the Whole Family,* which was available in five languages. He also made a film on New Games for Swedish television. Since that time, Dale has produced videos, CD-ROMS, and lately, DVDs to complement the New Games books. To find out more about these, check the Resources section of this book, and for a lot more detail, look at the New Games website: www.inewgames.com

Acknowledgments

The author and publisher would like to acknowledge the following for permission to quote from their work:

Quote from *To Hear the Angels Sing* by Dorothy Maclean, ©1980, reprinted by permission of the Findhorn Foundation.

Quote from the *Tao Te Ching* by Lao Tsu reprinted by permission of Alfred A. Knopf, Inc.

Quotes from *Zen Mind, Beginners Mind* by Shunryu Suzuki, ©1973, reprinted by permission of John Weatherhill, Inc.

Quote from *The Animals Came in One by One* by Buster Lloyd-Jones, ©1986, reprinted by permission of Martin Secker & Warburg Limited.

Quote from *Stranger in a Strange Land* by Robert A. Heinlein, ©1961, published by Putnams, reprinted by permission of Robert A. Heinlein.

Quote from *The Seth Material* by Jane Roberts, ©1970, reprinted by permission of Prentice Hall Press.

Quote from *Finite and Infinite Games* by James P. Carse, ©1986, reprinted by permission of The Free Press, a Division of Macmillan, Inc.

Quote from "Metalogue: About Games and Being Serious" by Gregory Bateson first appeared in *ETC: A Review of General Semantics,* Vol. X, No. 3 (1953), reprinted by permission of the International Society of General Semantics.

Quote from *The Mind of Clover* by Robert Aitken, ©1984, published by North Point Press and reprinted by permission.

I am grateful to the following people for their assistance in the writing of this book:

Ray Wilkins, Crete, Greece

Shoshana Tembeck, Oakland, California

Barbara Naiditch, San Francisco, California

Jill Iggulden, Cape Town, South Africa

Anne Lavelle, Amsterdam, Holland

Todd Strong, San Francisco, California

Sabine Weeke, Findhorn, Scotland

Barbara Adler, Copenhagen, Demmark

Note: illustration of Dale on page 154 is by Sanna Koski, Fort Bragg, CA USA 95437

Photography:

Adriana Sjan Bijman, Findhorn, Scotland: pp. xiv, 4, 10, 92 (both), 101

David Cairns, Forres, Scotland: pp. 42, 72

Bill Carter, Bombay, India: pp. 58, 119

Duo Bogforlaget staff photographs, Denmark: pp. 41, 66

Per Frisk, Stockholm, Sweden, pp. 17, 22, 24 (top), 32, 43, 45 (top, bottom), 65, 74 (bottom), 77, 80, 81, 82 (bottom), 85, 87, 90, 91, 93, 100 (top, bottom), 103, 109, 110, 117

Natalie Goldsmith, Durban, Republic of South Africa: pp. v, 7, 8, 13, 24 (bottom), 26, 39, 49, 56, 59 (top, bottom), 71, 89, 104

InnerLinks, USA: p. 131

InnerLinks, United Kingdon: p. 132

Rennie Innis, Findhorn, Scotland: p. 16

Sverre Koxvold, Forres, Scotland: pp. ii, iv (top, middle), 20 (both), 29, 30 (all), 31 (both), 38, 40 (bottom), 44, 57, 60, 64, 67, 75, 82 (top), 88, 94, 107, 128, 140

Dale Le Fevre, Adelaide, Australia: pp. 30 (middle), 46, 47

Keith Marcum, San Francisco, California: pp. 27, 86

O Books, Berkeley, USA for permission to reproduce the cover of
    The Quest: p. 137

Virginia Poole, Sitia, Crete, Greece: p. 68

Claudette Renner, Stockholm, Sweden: pp. 102, 158

Virginia Sajan, San Francisco, California: pp. iv (bottom), 23, 33,
    61, 62

Ruediger Voss, Geneva, Switzerland: p. 120 (top, bottom)

Christian Wopp, Oldenburg, Germany: pp. 84 (top, bottom)

Developmental Skills Section:

Diederich Sielken and Ursula Jakobs, Cologne, Germany

The nature of mind
the mind of god
the mind of the Christ,
Buddha, Mohammed,
Yahweh and all
true teachers
is my mind
is your mind.

We are all god
if we are but ready
to look within
and see ourselves
as we really are.

April 29, 2007
Dale

Return to the beginning;

become a child again.

Tao Te Ching

FINDHORN PRESS

Books, Card Sets,
CDs & DVDs
that inspire and uplift

For a complete catalogue,
please contact:

Findhorn Press Ltd
305a The Park, Findhorn
Forres IV36 3TE
Scotland, UK

Telephone
+44-(0)1309-690582
Fax
+44-(0)1309-690036
eMail
info@findhornpress.com

or consult our catalogue online
(with secure order facility) on
www.findhornpress.com